# HIDE TREASURES

# NEWCASTLE

Edited by Katie Coles

First published in Great Britain in 2002 by
*YOUNG WRITERS*
Remus House,
Coltsfoot Drive,
Peterborough, PE2 9JX
Telephone (01733) 890066

HB ISBN 0 75433 766 9
SB ISBN 0 75433 767 7

# FOREWORD

This year, the Young Writers' Hidden Treasures competition proudly presents a showcase of the best poetic talent from over 72,000 up-and-coming writers nationwide.

Young Writers was established in 1991 and we are still successful, even in today's technologically-led world, in promoting and encouraging the reading and writing of poetry.

The thought, effort, imagination and hard work put into each poem impressed us all, and once again, the task of selecting poems was a difficult one, but nevertheless, an enjoyable experience.

We hope you are as pleased as we are with the final selection and that you and your family continue to be entertained with *Hidden Treasures Newcastle* for many years to come.

# CONTENTS

| | |
|---|---|
| Brendan Bennett | 15 |
| Matthew Rushton | 15 |
| Natasha Miller | 16 |
| Sarah J Burns | 16 |

## Chopwell Primary School

| | |
|---|---|
| Hannah Shepherdson | 16 |
| Siobhan Ramsay | 17 |
| Tom Walton | 17 |
| Rebecca Dixon | 17 |
| Danielle McKinnon | 18 |
| Bess Lynn | 18 |
| Natasha Bougourd | 19 |
| Jodie Reid | 20 |
| Laura Clears | 21 |
| Conor Douglas | 22 |
| Nicola Jobes | 23 |
| Abbie Halcro | 23 |
| Ben Morley | 24 |
| Darren Laverick | 24 |
| Jessica Nunn | 24 |
| Laura McNestry | 25 |
| Sam Peel | 25 |
| Natalie Brown | 26 |
| Daryl Wilkinson | 26 |
| Shannon Hagan | 27 |
| Carl Parker | 27 |
| Nicole Graham | 28 |
| Jonathan Roddham | 28 |
| Sophie Wilkinson | 29 |
| Carl Armstrong | 29 |
| Jessica Lomax | 30 |
| Dean Purvis | 30 |
| Holly Kilgour | 31 |
| Kristopher Richardson | 31 |
| April Graham | 32 |
| Jacob Dodds | 32 |
| Natasha Brown | 33 |

Clover Hill Commuity Primary School

| | |
|---|---|
| Georgia Hastie | 45 |
| Jaynie Brooks | 46 |
| Sam Swinhoe | 47 |
| David Hynman | 48 |
| Stephanie Longstaff | 48 |
| Ashlee Callaghan | 49 |
| Christopher Hillcox | 49 |
| Emma Stapleton | 50 |
| Sophie Cox | 50 |
| Lucy Zwolinska | 50 |
| Sanchia Andries | 51 |
| Shaun Batey | 51 |
| Craig Ainscough | 52 |
| Amber Case | 52 |
| Rachael Stillwell | 52 |
| Nicola Brown | 53 |
| Leanne Butler | 53 |
| Katy Martin | 54 |
| Craig Batey | 54 |
| James Knott | 54 |
| Elicia Hills | 55 |
| Connor Butler | 55 |
| Alex Clapham | 56 |
| Steven J Hall | 56 |
| Alexander Edward Hewson | 56 |
| Joshua Telfer | 57 |
| Katrina Powell | 57 |
| Heather Shaw | 58 |
| Hannah Lovatt | 58 |
| Michael Haig | 59 |
| Jennifer Mutch | 59 |
| Tony McMeiken | 60 |
| Lee Goldsbrough | 60 |
| Danielle Armstrong | 61 |
| Jason Bell | 61 |
| Amy Gray | 62 |
| Jayne Drummond | 62 |

| | |
|---|---|
| Jamie Barclay | 63 |
| Lucy Sage | 63 |
| Melissa Appleby | 64 |
| Craig M Green | 64 |
| Thomas Oliver Morrison | 65 |
| Danielle Cromarty | 65 |
| Sophie Delarny | 66 |
| Harvey Willis | 66 |
| Michael Brown | 67 |
| James Farrey | 67 |
| Bethany Walker | 68 |
| Michael Richardson | 68 |
| Serena Pacitti | 69 |
| Emma Smith | 69 |
| Michaela Forbes | 70 |
| Chelsey Mason | 70 |
| Carter Rippon | 71 |
| Kathryn Craig | 71 |
| Jamie Leech | 72 |
| John Richardson | 72 |
| Scott Swinhoe | 73 |
| Miriam Atkinson | 73 |
| Kathryn Tinson | 74 |
| Monique Kelsey | 74 |
| Peter Robson | 74 |
| Aaron Wilson | 75 |
| Serena Sahota | 75 |
| Catriona Bathan | 75 |
| Hannah McColl | 76 |
| Mark Ainsley | 76 |
| Hannah Whyte | 76 |
| Jessica Turner | 77 |
| Louise Morrod | 77 |
| Matthew Bracchi | 78 |
| Jennifer Brown | 78 |
| Jordan Hewitt | 79 |
| Ross Pembroke | 79 |

Cragside Primary School

| | |
|---|---|
| Casey Graham | 79 |
| Ashleigh Collins | 80 |
| Nikki Anderson | 81 |
| Daniel Holmes | 82 |
| Martin Hall | 82 |
| Thomas Foy | 83 |
| Emma Humphries | 84 |
| Victoria Canham | 84 |
| Roszeen Afsar | 85 |
| Heather Buchan | 86 |
| Emma Jobson | 86 |
| Leanne Bower | 87 |
| Alexandra Sinton | 88 |
| Jane Potts | 88 |
| Lisa Hardy | 89 |
| Andrew Wilkinson | 89 |
| Michael Keen | 90 |
| Sammy Bertram | 90 |
| Shaun Douglas | 91 |
| Louise Hutchinson | 91 |
| Louise Parr | 92 |
| Martin Anderson | 93 |
| Dan Scott | 93 |
| Leanne Kennedy | 94 |

Hawthorn Primary School

| | |
|---|---|
| Stephen Watson | 94 |

Ivy Road Primary School

| | |
|---|---|
| Sarah Horne | 94 |
| Sarah Husband | 95 |
| Charlie O'Brien | 95 |
| Andrew Jobling | 96 |
| Liam Dickson | 97 |
| Hayley Cameron | 98 |
| Amy Scott | 98 |

| | |
|---|---|
| David Riall | 99 |
| Jennifer Eastland | 99 |

La Sagesse Convent Junior School

| | |
|---|---|
| Eleanor Reynolds | 100 |
| Megan Roberts | 100 |
| Briony Duff | 101 |
| Madeleine Otter | 102 |
| Jennie Watson | 102 |
| Clella Middleton | 103 |
| Katie Crumbley | 104 |
| Francesca Ayre | 104 |
| Lucy O'Donnell | 105 |
| Claire Allen | 106 |
| Sabea Morgan | 106 |
| Hannah Abu-harb | 107 |
| Katherine Gibb | 108 |
| Genevieve Crozier | 108 |
| Jessica Major | 109 |
| Naomi Hicks | 110 |
| Beth Watson | 111 |
| Daisy Abraham | 112 |
| Megan Dale | 113 |
| Rebecca Hsu Webb-Mitchell | 114 |
| Jessica McClean | 114 |
| Abbie Bowman | 115 |
| Natalie-Emma Weatherley | 115 |
| Jessica Hall | 116 |
| Charlotte Bennetts | 116 |
| Lucy Jobson | 117 |
| Chloe Grace Cullen | 117 |
| Martha Craven | 118 |
| Emma Blackshaw | 118 |
| Sophia Spiropoulos | 119 |
| Rachael Gourley | 119 |
| Katie Gilfillan | 120 |
| Emma Donohoe | 120 |
| Amy Smith | 121 |

*The Poems*

# THE BLUE ALIEN

The ugly, big alien, blue as the sea
hovered across burning buildings
like flicking a fly
The alien started
to kick shops down
like kicking a football
then he started bending lampposts
He ran down town
and he took the king's crown
The alien had enough fun for one day
so he got back in his spaceship
and *zoooooomed* away.

*Jamie Moffat (9)*
*Balliol Primary School*

# AUTUMN

Frosty, followed by leaves
Trees which are amber-brown
And yellow leaves around the flowers
Nice and dry
When crushed by hands
Nice colours
Cool and lovely
To see in a book.

*Laura Spry (7)*
*Balliol Primary School*

## FOOTBALL

Football, football, I love football
Don't forget to kick the ball in the goal
Football, football, don't get dirty
Stay clean, stay good at football
Impress your trainer
It's starting to rain, go inside
Get a drink, dry yourself off
I can see a rainbow
There it is, shining its bright colours.

*Becki Colquhoun  (9)*
*Balliol Primary School*


## MY ANIMAL POEM

A   nimals are gentle
N   aughty
I    ntelligent
M  ucky
A   dorable
L   oving
S   cary.

*James Muckle  (9)*
*Balliol Primary School*


## ICE CREAM

Ice cream, ice cream, I love you so much
I would even eat you if I was Dutch
You are the greatest thing that happened to me
Is it all right if I call you *icy creamy*

Your creamy top head
Your crunchy cone of a body
Your creamy heads, crunchy body
*Is truly the best that happened to me!*

***Jack Blackett (9)***
***Balliol Primary School***


## FOOD

Chips and pizza on a plate
They always make me want to skate

I like my veg
And when I've had them I crawl through the hedge

I like sausage and beans
And I also like Newcastle football team.

***Paula Nanson (9)***
***Balliol Primary School***


## THANASIE POEM

T hanasie
H ouse cleaner
A nnoying
N otey
A ngry
S illy
I ndependent
E nergetic.

***Thanasie Lambros (10)***
***Balliol Primary School***

## MONSTER, MONSTER!

Monster, monster
Ugly monster
Monster, monster
Spiky monster
Monster, monster
Hairy monster
Monster, monster
In my dumpster
What will I do?
Get a torch
Monster, monster
In my basement
Monster, monster
*I'm scared!*

*Aaron Hassain  (8)*
*Balliol Primary School*

## OH BEAST

Oh beast, oh beast, I'm not scared
What is your name?
Oh child
Oh child, my name is Minotaur
I have red fiery eyes, big sharp teeth and big horns
Oh no!
I'm very scared
To tell you the truth
I'm very scared.

*Adam Wilson  (7)*
*Balliol Primary School*

## OLD MISS HUBBERD

Old Miss Hubberd
Went to the cupboard
And saw that the cupboard was bare
Her dog made a groan
And she started to moan
And then she went to pick up the phone.

She picked it up and phoned the dog pound
And they took the poor dog away
The dog was never seen again.

The poor old woman went back to the cupboard
And wished that she had food
She opened the cupboard and saw plenty of food
'Come back,' she said
She really liked that dog.

*Daniel Charters  (10)*
*Balliol Primary School*

## BILLY BELLY

Billy Belly wore a welly
While he watched the telly
He spied some jelly on his belly
Then the telly went off
He saw the telly in his jelly
He dropped the jelly in the telly
That did not satisfy Billy Belly.

*Dean Patterson  (9)*
*Balliol Primary School*

## SCARY MONSTERS

Scary monsters
Black and white
Red and blue
Squelchy and slimy
Hard and cracking
Some are scary, some are not
Some hurt humans but some don't
Some don't care
One monster is stupid
The rest are not
Some steal off humans, some don't
Some are cool dudes, some are not.

*Sarah May  (7)*
*Balliol Primary School*

## THE MOON

The moon was as bright as day
It shone through the cold night when night was over
The moon fell down with a mighty smash
The stars looked down with excitement
The stars said, 'Yippee, the moon is dead'
The moon looked up
And howled like a wolf
A spaceship came with a zoom
To take the big lump of cheese away.

*Amberley Holmes  (8)*
*Balliol Primary School*

## MY AUNTIE LOUISE

My auntie Louise,
Was a horrible lass,
She baked her,
Husband in the
Oven with a cat.

He's far too nice,
To boil or cook,
She cooked him,
Into a giant foot.

But then later that week,
She was so neat,
She put ma into the oven with her mother,
And cooked another.

*Ashleigh Overdon  (10)*
*Balliol Primary School*


## AUTUMN

Sometimes snowy, cold and rainy
And sometimes frosty
Dark clouds rush across the sky
Foggy, windy and chilly
And sometimes sunny.

*Christopher Rushton  (8)*
*Balliol Primary School*


## AUTUMN

Autumn is cold and rainy
It is chilly
The screeching owl
Rushing across the sky.

*Cheryl Lascelles  (7)*
*Balliol Primary School*

# DON'T DO THAT!

Don't do that, don't do that!

Don't put flies in your eyes
Don't put beer in your ear

Don't do that, don't do that!

Don't bang your head on the bed
Don't put peas on the TVs

Don't do that, don't do that!

Don't hit the hen with the pen
Don't eat the jelly and fill you your belly

Don't do that!

*Melissa Drummond  (11)*
*Balliol Primary School*

# I'M SCARED

I'm scared, there's not a single person about
I'm scared, I dream of a monster in my bed
*I'm scared!*
I tiptoe out of the house
I look down and there's a mouse
Nibbling at my toes
I run away, scared
I see a monster in the street
*I'm scared!*

*Ryan Woolley  (7)*
*Balliol Primary School*

## MY UNCLE JOHN

My Uncle John was a terrible man
He fried his wife and cat in the frying pan
But they were far too sweet and tender to eat
So in a flash they were in the dustbin with the toys
So after a while he fried an egg
But he was so angry he fried it into a chick again.

*Joanne Jobson (10)*
*Balliol Primary School*


## THE BLACK MONSTER

Monster, monster, he's so terrifying
Monster, monster, he's so big
Monster, monster, he's so ugly
Monster, monster, he's so mad
The monster was as terrifying as thousands of nightmares
He bit a human in half like a biscuit.

*Daniel Harrington (8)*
*Balliol Primary School*


## THERE'S A MONSTER UNDER MY BED

There's a monster under my bed
There's a monster under my bed
How could it be? I can't find him anywhere
Please! Please! Help me find him
I can't find him on my own.

*Samantha Skelton (8)*
*Balliol Primary School*

## FOXES

Their pointy ears and white sharp teeth
Make them look all cruel
But their big eyes make them look cute.
Their orange fur looks like fire
And the white fur looks like snow.
They are extremely cunning when they are hungry.
It's the fox, cute and cuddly but very dangerous.

*Rachael Hunter  (10)*
*Balliol Primary School*


## BIRDS TWEET WORDS

Albert albatross has an Australian accent
Bertie blackbird blabs
Colin crow is very confident in what he says and does
Derek duck is too dippy to speak
Eric emu explains everything.

*Amy Patterson  (9)*
*Balliol Primary School*


## MONSTER, MONSTER

Monster, monster
I hate you
Because the sound you make is so poor
Now the sound has disappeared
All is calm and windy too.

*Natasha Yarr  (8)*
*Balliol Primary School*

## RELAXATION

Don't get stressed
Rainbow blazing high and bright
Sunshine high in the sky
Shadows in the sparkly water
Dolphins swimming happily
Glitter dropping from the sky
Kids playing with ice - ice skates everywhere
Snow dropping
The kids notice the sparkly ground
Relax, don't get mad
People sitting in deck chairs staring at the sky
Peace everywhere
A person says, 'This is the life!'
At night-time you can see the horizon,
Relax!

*Abigail Dodds  (9)*
*Balliol Primary School*

## MONSTER, MONSTER

Monster, monster turn around
Monster, monster
Touch the ground
Monster, monster hear the sound
Monster, monster
I'm off home
To ready my secret bedtime poem.

*Shannon Etherington  (7)*
*Balliol Primary School*

## DON'T DO THAT

Don't do, don't do, don't do that!

Don't eat the fluff out your belly.
Don't drink the rum or eat the jelly.

Don't do, don't do, don't do that!

Don't put the tele on.
Don't eat the chocolate scone.

Don't do, don't do, don't do that!
Ding dong!

Go answer the door
But you said don't do, don't do, don't do that!

*Caroline Richardson  (11)*
*Balliol Primary School*


## WEATHER

Rain - drip-drop, slither, splashing on the rooftops
And splashing in streams.
Clouds - dull, grey, upsetting clouds
Ugly, dark clouds.
Sun - bright, happy sun, sparkling
But turns off at night.
Wind - howling, screaming, banging windows and doors
Smashing and snapping tiles and trees in half.
Snow - crinching, crunching, slish, slosh, skiing in the snow
And sledging through the streets.

*Craig Spring  (9)*
*Balliol Primary School*

## BUSY DAY

Buses like fish swimming along the road
Candyfloss clouds floating in the sky
Whilst being pecked at by birds flying by
Friendly trees waving their arms in the wind
Walking down the stairs into a monster's open mouth
Sinking deep into your pillow like a fluffy marshmallow
Goodnight!

*Claire Carden  (11)*
*Balliol Primary School*


## SCIENCE FICTION POEM

The robot with gigantic hooks clanked through the city
Picking up cars and throwing them like snowballs into buildings
The robot lifted a building off the ground and threw it into a dump yard
It blew up, it was as explosive as a supernova
The car leads the robot to the motorway
Jerked and the robot fell in the water.

*Liam Sherwood  (8)*
*Balliol Primary School*


## MARY

Mary had a little bear, she also had a frog
She went out to shop before she had some pop
And left a moustache on her mouth
She took in her plate and said, 'I want some dinner'
The bear looked at Mary's mouth then he ran out of the house
And never came back again.

*Aron Hall  (10)*
*Balliol Primary School*

## SCHOOL JUNGLE

Doors are going to gobble you up like a pie
Pubs are ready to swallow you up and spit you out

Rooftops are shaking like a leaf in the air
Air vents are steaming with anger

Traffic lights are like fruity lollies
They want you to press their button so you can lick them
Youth club wants you to play with it and tickle it.

*Aliesha King (10)*
*Balliol Primary School*


## HUSBAND

Husband, husband where have you been?
Where do you think, down the drain.

Husband, husband what is the time?
Just hang your knickers on the line.

Husband, husband where's my bed?
Where do you think, on my head.

*Nattasha Spry (10)*
*Balliol Primary School*


## OLD MAN RIVER

Old man river shivered and shivered
Until he could shiver no more
He sat in the bath which was pretty daft
Then he shivered no more.

*Kyle Hussain (10)*
*Balliol Primary School*

## FOOTBALL

F ootball match
O wen misses a great chance
O 'Brien scores a goal
T errible hack by Gerard
B ounces off the post
A ngry Shearer
L ovely goal Bellamy
L ovely crowd for Newcastle.

*Nick Dodds (10)*
*Balliol Primary School*


## SCHOOL POEM

S chool is boring
C ooking class if worse
H istory is alright
O liver is my best friend
O h Ryan is alright
L ibby is a twerp.

*Brendan Bennett (9)*
*Balliol Primary School*


## CANDY

C andy is a cute, cuddly cat and
A dorable
N utter
D ark and a
Y oung cat.

*Matthew Rushton (9)*
*Balliol Primary School*

## HAMSTER

A hamster is soft and warm
A hamster is furry and lovely
My hamster is clever
She is called Rollo
She likes to taste food
At Easter she gets an egg
Rollo is special
She is very cuddly and warm
She snuggles up with me.

*Natasha Miller  (10)*
*Balliol Primary School*


## DOGS

I love dogs
They're unlike logs
They run about all day
And sometimes they don't do what their owners say
I think this is what they stand for

D   isaster (all the time)
O   bedient (sometimes)
G   entle (sometimes).

*Sarah J Burns  (9)*
*Balliol Primary School*


## HAIKU

Fish splash water high
Baby wolves bite hard and growl
Moose tackle others.

*Hannah Shepherdson  (8)*
*Chopwell Primary School*

## SCHOOL

S    chool is
C    ool sometimes
H    omework is hard
O    ops! My pencil slipped
O    ops! I made a mistake
L    iteracy is fun.

*Siobhan Ramsay  (8)*
*Chopwell Primary School*


## SCHOOL

S    chool
C    lass
H    olidays are great
'O   tten tables test
'O   tten lumpy potatoes
L    ollipop lady off sick.

*Tom Walton  (8)*
*Chopwell Primary School*


## SCHOOL

S    cience is
C    ool
H    omework is hard
O    h, oh! Maths test
O    h, oh! Soggy cabbage
L    iteracy is the best.

*Rebecca Dixon  (8)*
*Chopwell Primary School*

## WHAT A NIGHTMARE!

I went to class
I wished I hadn't
While I was on holiday
The basement had crumbled
My teacher was there
Oh no, oh my!
Oh yes, someone had come in
Oh, it was Conor
I had a dream about him last night
He fell down a hole
And our teacher saved his life
I could not believe a word of this
Sam had given Conor a kiss
Oh, hip hip hooray
Natalie came
She's spilt the water all over the place
Oh no, oh my beautiful hair
She jumped round, just chilling round
She was singing 'Byker Grove', oh no
We were doing short division
I felt sorry for long division
Those poor children in 1950
Amie came eventually, she saved me from the head
Well, not really
*What a nightmare!*

*Danielle McKinnnon  (10)*
*Chopwell Primary School*


## BAGS

Bags I the dummy
Bags I the cot
Bags I the rubber duck
That's out of the baby's cot

Bags I the cricket ball
Wickets and bats
Bags I the hamster
Bags I the cat.

*Bess Lynn  (10)*
*Chopwell Primary School*


## FANCY DRESS

It's the 31st October and fancy dress day at school
Conor's dressed up as a mule
Laura Clears is a little ugly duck
Natalie looks like an old crook!

Jodie is a frog prince
Nicola is a pie of mince
John is a fig
And Carl's wearing a pink wig!

Sam H is a pig
Sam P is an earwig
Laura M is a warty warlock
And Glen's a door lock!

Andrew is a mummy
Dannielle is a dummy
Kate is a corpse
And Michelle has warts!

Dane is an old lady
Amie is Sadie
Miss Marsh is a rotten apple core
And Mr Grey is Dumbledore.

*Natasha Bougourd  (10)*
*Chopwell Primary School*

## THE WEIRD DAY

It was fancy dress in our school
And John is dressed up like a swimming pool

While Conor is in his silk dress
Natasha is wearing a pink skirt, ugh what a mess!

Natalie's hair is green (and it looks better than normal)
While some infant's mouth is covered in ice cream

Laura Clears looks as if she is going in a huff
And Dane is wearing some fake muscles to look tough

Andrew is dressed as Hitler again
And Natasha with her pink skirt is driving the teacher insane!

Kate has become a mad snake
And Laura McNestry has become a sweet chocolate cake, mmm!

Amie Ramsay is just bored out of his wits
And Andrew is talking about the Blitz

Mark has become a dog
Nicola has turned Michelle into a frog!

Sam Peel has a girl squeal
Sam Hardy is Frankenstein
And Carl is a washing line

Danielle is a cat
Glen is a viscous rat!

The teachers look horrendous
My teacher is a pirate and she looks tremendous

But something is wrong, all these outfits are gruesome
Is it Hallowe'en? It is!

I looked stupid because I had to get ready quick and I went home
That is why I am not in this poem.

*Jodie Reid  (10)*
*Chopwell Primary School*


## TEACHER'S DIARY

It's snowing in the playground
And just look what I've found
A diary so pink and fluffy
Without a sound I go and tell Muffy
We open it at page two
It says Mr Spotty I love you

I've just seen something that caught my eye
It says I want to go out with Mr Chatty
But I'm too shy

It says Miss Marsh
Is really harsh
And I agree with that
It says I had a talk with Miss Makeup
And it ended up a boring chat

And then it goes on about how silly kids are
And that she thinks we come from afar
Now here's something weird
I've been stealing make-up from my nana
Because I can't afford my own
From little Miss Spanner.

*Laura Clears  (9)*
*Chopwell Primary School*

## WEIRD SURPRISES

At my school today,
Everything is weird.
Everyone's in costume-
Miss Marsh has a beard!

Natalie's an old man;
Laura's Bob the Builder;
Natasha is Dracula
And Jodie is Matilda.

Nicola's a gargoyle;
Mark is Santa Claus;
Kate is a phantom -
Michelle and Kirsty have claws.

Carl and Glen are dragons;
Andrew is a dog;
Danielle's a wicked witch
And Laura M's a warthog

Sam H, a chicken, John's Frankenstein;
Amy is a headless zombie.
Sam P is an astro alien
And Dane is just plain dotty.

A monk, a Jedi, a mad man,
A Dumbledore and a Frodo.
The head was Prof McGonagle -
People in costume walked to and fro.

When I was going home,
My granddad had seen
That I had no costume
And told me, *'It's Hallowe'en!'*

*Conor Douglas  (10)*
*Chopwell Primary School*

## LATE AND EXCUSE CONVERSATION

Late again Bugtroter
What's the excuse this time?
Mam and dad, dead
Died!
Had to live with grandmamma
Now this is the way it goes
Mark's a hoy
Miss Mine is a pool table
Laura's a book
Kate's a mate
Has it finished yet?
Yes
Why were you late yesterday?
My sister fell down the stairs
My dentist fainted
My mum's sister broke her leg
Kit young man?
No
Why?
Where's you kit now?
Dead.

*Nicola Jobes  (9)*
*Chopwell Primary School*


## HAIKU

The wind is blowing
The river is swaying fast
The storm is whistling.

*Abbie Halcro*
*Chopwell Primary School*

## BIG BEN CLOCK

He stands tall and proud
With a tan
He has one face
He has two hands
He can see all the way to Japan
He has twelve eyes
His organs go tick tock every second
His heart goes ding dong
Tick tock, tick tock goes the Big Ben clock.

*Ben Morley (11)*
*Chopwell Primary School*


## SCHOOL

S chool is
C ool but
H omework I don't know
O ops! I broke a window
O h no, the head wants to see me
L ove school really.

*Darren Laverick (9)*
*Chopwell Primary School*


## HAIKU

Here comes the winter
I love the winter snow deep
Time to wrap up warm.

*Jessica Nunn (8)*
*Chopwell Primary School*

## TWINS

I've got a twin in my class
He's a pain in the neck
Flicking things around
While the rest of them are sound.

Just the same with his twin
He used to be as silent as a pin
But I think he's had a spell on him.

Do you know what he did yesterday?
He was flicking pencils all over the place
So what did you do?
Told the head of course!

And what did she say?
She said
'They can't be in this school
No way!'

*Laura McNestry (10)*
*Chopwell Primary School*

## SCHOOL

Why didn't Mum send me to a decent school
Where the roofs don't leak
And the floorboards don't creak
Where teachers rule
Instead of drool
In the old barn there is a mule
And the caretaker is a fool.

*Sam Peel (10)*
*Chopwell Primary School*

## FANCY DRESS DAY

Here I am, school again
It's fancy dress day, please help me!

My mother says it's best to be Cinderella
Oh dear me!
I'm a boy, how bad can you get?

But then again I could have been in a frilly pink dress
Miss Marsh is Dumbo
Her ears are jumbo
But then again, she looks nice
A little make-up and she'll be all right
But then again make-up is not her style.

*Natalie Brown  (10)*
*Chopwell Primary School*


## MY BROTHER SILVEST

My brother Silvest
He's got about forty medals on his chest
*Big chest!*
He's got an arm like a leg and a punch like dynamite
He thought he'd take a trip to Italy
And he'd take a trip out to sea
He saw the Titanic in distress
So he hoisted the Titanic on his chest
And that was the end of my brother Silvest.

*Daryl Wilkinson  (11)*
*Chopwell Primary School*

## LOSING FRIENDS AND MAKING FRIENDS

Spss, spss
Spss, spss, that's what friends do
Talk here, talk there
Never shut up
Lose a friend
Make a friend
That's what friends do

Ha ha
Hee hee, that's what new friends do
New friends make me laugh
Giggle here
Giggle there
That's what new friends do

Punch, kick
Slam, bonk
That's what old friends do
Yell, shout
Scream, whisper
That's what old friends do.

*Shannon Hagan (11)*
*Chopwell Primary School*


## BEN AND THE HEN

There was a boy called Ben
Who was married to a hen
The hen died
Ben cried
And then he married a wren.

*Carl Parker (10)*
*Chopwell Primary School*

## MY DOG

My dog is going to beat the rest,
She might be a pest,
But she's still the best,
Her name is going to be Tess,
Tess will never let me down,
Tess will never runaway from me,
While down in the town,
We go on the bus,
She sits on my lap on the way home,
Cry, cry, cry, is all I hear,
We get back, she goes to her food bowl,
I feed her, her favourite food 'Chump',
Tess then goes to bed,
And dreams of all the days that are ahead of her.

*Nicole Graham  (10)*
*Chopwell Primary School*

## FOOTBALL

F   igo is the best footballer in the world
O   wn goals count
O   wen plays for Liverpool
T   all people are a bit faster
B   all boys get the ball when it goes out
A   ndrew O'Brien has got a big nose
L   ying gets you nowhere when you hack someone
L   ying might get you a yellow card and these are some tactics
     about football.

*Jonathan Roddham  (10)*
*Chopwell Primary School*

# WALKING THROUGH THE FAIRGROUND

Walking through the fairground
Pop goes the balloon
Walking through the fairground
I know you
Walking through the fairground
Round the carousel
Walking through the fairground
Pink candyfloss
Walking through the fairground
I feel sick
Walking through the fairground
You're all pink
Walking through the fairground
Fuzz goes the can
Walking
    through
        through
            through
                the fairground!

*Sophie Wilkinson (11)*
*Chopwell Primary School*


# THE MAN FROM ROME

There was a man from Rome
Who swallowed a great big comb
The doctor came quick
The man felt sick
And now he lives in a home.

*Carl Armstrong (11)*
*Chopwell Primary School*

## WALKING THROUGH THE PLAYGROUND

Walking through the playground
*Smash*
*Crash*
*Bang*
'Ouch, get off me!'
'Head teacher, both of you!'
Walking through the playground
'White shoe, white shoe'
'Leave me alone'
Punch, punch, kick
Walking through the playground
Bounce, bounce no!
*'Stupid!'*
'I've got Polos'
'I'm snitching'
'Don't'
'Ding dong'.

*Jessica Lomax  (11)*
*Chopwell Primary School*


## NEWCASTLE

Newcastle are the best
Newcastle score goals
Newcastle don't lose
Shearer is the best
They are going to win the FA Cup
So watch out
Newcastle are about.

*Dean Purvis  (10)*
*Chopwell Primary School*

## MY NAME

H   ad chips for tea last night.
O   ranges are my favourite fruit.
L   ollies are nice in the summer.
L   ooking at clothes is my second best thing.
Y   our bed is nice and cosy.

R   abbits are my favourite pets.
A   nd my best food is chips.
C   hristine is my mam's name.
H   olly is my name.
E   rnie is my dad's name.
L   ooking at shoes is my favourite thing.

K   ay is my cousin.
I   love my boyfriend.
L   oving people is very nice.
G   oing on holiday is very exciting.
O   ur families are like our friends.
U   nhappy is not very nice to be.
R   ats I do not like.

*Holly Kilgour  (8)*
*Chopwell Primary School*


## DINOSAUR

The thirty-foot killer, the blood spiller,
bone breaker, flesh cutter,
tree smasher, life ender,
scaly skin, long legs,
powerful claws, predator.

*Kristopher Richardson  (10)*
*Chopwell Primary School*

## A Funny Poem

A    bsent April
P    erfect April
R    acing April
I    cy April
L    aughing April

G    orilla April
R    ainbow April
A    pril the ape
H    andy April
A    ttached April
M    oody April.

*April Graham  (8)*
*Chopwell Primary School*


## Jacob Dodds

J    acob I am, yes Jacob I am
A    nd I am crazy about football
C    an't do basketball, can't do netball
O    h I'm crazy about football
B    all in the net, ball in the net

D    odds is a dude
O    r Dodds is daft
D    odds is good or
D    odds is bad
S    uch a silly boy he is.

*Jacob Dodds  (8)*
*Chopwell Primary School*

## A TERRIBLE NIGHT

I wake up,
With a scare,
What can I hear?
My sister snores,
I toss I turn,
It's dark and scary
The owls hoot!
The stairs creak,
I kick the bed,
I'm hot, boiling hot.
I sleep, a horrible dream,
A ghost trying to get me!
I wake up,
My mum shouts 'Natasha'
I think, good,
Morning is here,
What a terrible night!

*Natasha Brown (10)*
*Chopwell Primary School*


## DOLPHINS

Dolphins come in all different species
Bottle-nosed, Atlantic-spotted and even common dolphins
Jumping through the waves
Day in, day out
I wish I could be a dolphin
As blue as the sky.

*Jill Shepherd (10)*
*Chopwell Primary School*

## OH NO YOU'RE SHAN

My mam said 'It's time to come in,'
Oh no you're shan,

My mam said 'It's time for your bath,'
Oh no you're shan,

My dad said 'It's time for bed,'
Oh no you're shan,

My gran said 'It's time to get up for school,'
Oh no you're shan,

My dad said 'You're grounded tonight,'
Oh no you're shan,

I walked home from school head hung low
Ready to tell them they're shan.

Oh no so cool - it's my birthday
A new bike - you're so great.

*Kelly Aiston (9)*
*Chopwell Primary School*


## MY STUNT HAMSTER

My hamster is a fur ball
She is a stunt girl
She is an exercise girl
And a mad girl
She's a hamster
*A stunt hamster!*

*Anthony Parker (10)*
*Chopwell Primary School*

## THE TWINS!

The twins are fighting and biting
The twins are mad and bad
The twins are nipping and kicking
The twins are teasing and squeezing
The twins are best at being a pest.

*Claire Louise Queen  (10)*
*Chopwell Primary School*


## WIND

The wind is
Wild
The wind is
Calm
The wind is
Loud
As loud as an
*Alarm!*

*Michael Robson  (10)*
*Chopwell Primary School*


## THERE WAS A YOUNG MAN CALLED DEAN

There was a young man called Dean
Who ate a lot of beans
He ate a mint
But he was then skint
And he became very mean.

*John Gainford  (11)*
*Chopwell Primary School*

## THE REGISTER

I am starting the register
Right, shut up!
Amy Belter
Billie Wattie
Be quiet
Danielle Numter
David Litter
I am giving you five seconds
5, 4, 3, 2, 1, right
Ella Marsh
George Wallie
Isabella Notterle
Jessica Longstapj

Katie Tuney
Nicole Gragey
That's it, go out
I am fed up with your stupid behaviour
*Billie!* Get out
I mean it, don't try my patience
Okay now, let's get on with it
Olivia Waterman
Sophie Wattle
Phew!
Thank goodness you're quiet
Liam take this down to the reception desk and hurry
You don't want to miss PE!

*Rowanna Marston  (11)*
*Chopwell Primary School*

## THINK

Think you are lucky - yes, you and me
Think of people in Africa that have nothing to eat
No clean water to drink and hardly any clothes to wear
Think you are lucky - yes, you and me
Think you are lucky
What is the world to be?
Think you are lucky
There are poor people out there
So just don't stand and stare.

*Katie Welsh  (11)*
*Chopwell Primary School*


## BUTTERFLY

Butterfly, butterfly
How lucky you are
You fly high in the sky
You see clouds and stars
You see rivers and forests
Butterfly, butterfly
How lucky you are.

*Anastasia Levynskaya  (10)*
*Chopwell Primary School*


## HAIKU

The wind is blowing
The grass is flowing today
Children are shouting.

*Dale Armstrong  (8)*
*Chopwell Primary School*

## HORSES

My friend used to have a horse,
She named it Bonnie,
Bonnie was a little rascal and a little pest.
My other friend has a horse called Pennie,
Pennie is a beauty,
Pennie is palomino and a cross with a Dunn,
When it is night they say goodnight,
There are so many breeds,
Some are small and some are very big.

*Danielle Lowe  (11)*
*Chopwell Primary School*


## MANHATTAN

The Hudson river running beside it
Maddison Square Gardens in the centre of it
The Empire State building, the biggest thing in it
The Trade Center rumbled straight up Fifth Avenue.

*John Keogan  (10)*
*Chopwell Primary School*


## DAN

There was a young man called Dan
Who got hit with a pan
He went back to school
And got called a fool
And never went back again.

*Daniel Fox  (10)*
*Chopwell Primary School*

## THE TRAVELLING TEACHER

The travelling teacher which is my mum
She goes to schools all over the globe
And she's got a big bum
Once I said 'Mum what should I say?
A girl at school is asking me out'
'Just say 'Oui' for I have been
To the City of Love AKA Paris.

*Carl Jackson (10)*
*Chopwell Primary School*


## MY FOOTBALL PITCH

You can't see my football pitch,
My football pitch is in the air.
There are no people just me and my friend,
Also there are secret passages.

You can jump higher than you thought,
All of a sudden someone went in a passage and disappeared.

But the best thing is you can play any time you want.

*Niki Shepherd (10)*
*Chopwell Primary School*


## HAIKU

Soft soothing water
Fish swimming around inside
Raindrops blowing by.

*Rhys Liddle (9)*
*Chopwell Primary School*

## JORDAN

J ordan was a very good swimmer
O r very good at tennis
R avens beat her brother
D angerous mines she goes into
A nd there is no fear
N o sweat, no fear, no sissy girls.

*Jordan May Eadington (8)*
*Chopwell Primary School*


## DANIEL

D aniel is good at football
A nd good at tennis
N othing was wrong
I was good at mini golf
E very day I play sport
L ovely football.

*Daniel Burlinson (8)*
*Chopwell Primary School*


## THE ROB

R aggie Robert robbed the bank.
O oo the police are coming.
B etter start running
E ee you stop right there!
R obbing the branch it was not me.
T oo true you were.

*Robert Strong (8)*
*Chopwell Primary School*

## KELSIE

K elsie was quite good at maths
E nglish was a bit easier.
L iked to use the scales,
S he liked to do some history.
I enjoy doing art
E nd of the day.

*Kelsie Hodgson (7)*
*Chopwell Primary School*


## DANIEL SHIPLEY

D aniel was very good at drawing
A nd also very talented in football
'N othing you can't do,' his dad used to say
'I 'm very good at mini-golf too'
E veryone thought he was the best at drawing in class
'L ovely football.'

*Daniel Shipley (7)*
*Chopwell Primary School*


## THE GYMNAST

She jumps as high as a grasshopper
High as the sky,
I really believe she thinks she can fly.
She runs as fast as a cheetah,
As sleek as a cat.
The gymnast.

*Amie Meadows (10)*
*Chopwell Primary School*

# A Cat's Day

She comes through the cat flap after a very long night,
Expecting her breakfast as soon as it gets light.
She goes into the garden and dozes on the wall,
A couple of hours later she gets up to stretch so tall.
She strolls into the kitchen to wolf down her fill,
Then gracefully laps her milk up, so as not to make a spill.
So now back into the dark of the street,
Away from the comfort of my mum's feet.
And out in the street she likes to stay,
Until the break of the very next day.

*Amy Bradford  (10)*
*Chopwell Primary School*

# Icarus

I    carus is the son of Deadalus
C   rete is the country he went to
A   pair of wings is what he made
R   an away is what he did
U   p and up is where he went
S   un is what burnt him.

*Adam James  (8)*
*Chopwell Primary School*

# Haiku

A good, happy day
Under the tall Christmas tree
A great day it was.

*Katie Anne Harbord  (9)*
*Chopwell Primary School*

## HAIKU

The wind blows strong and
The river flows gently by
The grass swishes green.

*Christopher Black  (8)*
*Chopwell Primary School*


## HAIKU

The wind blows up hard
It goes up and down, fast and strong
It blows me around.

*Ashleigh Peacock  (9)*
*Chopwell Primary School*


## HAIKU

The wins are blowing
Rabbits playing in the sun,
I like seeing them.

*Jane Conchie  (8)*
*Chopwell Primary School*


## MATHS

Adds, divisions, times and take aways,
You've got to stick in at maths.
That's what my mam always says.

*Nicole Dunn  (10)*
*Chopwell Primary School*

## HAIKU

Spiders spiders scared
They are horrid crawly
Big hairy and black.

*Rachel Deary  (9)*
*Chopwell Primary School*


## HAIKU

Orange and blue
Sky ablaze burning red glow
It is like fire.

*Dean Byers  (8)*
*Chopwell Primary School*


## HAIKU

The blazing fire
Glows lighter and brave so strong
Orange, red all day.

*Michael Nathan Blakemore  (8)*
*Chopwell Primary School*


## HAIKU

Teachers are talking
They are drinking their coffee
The school bell rings, *No!*

*Adam Mansfield  (9)*
*Chopwell Primary School*

## MY FOOTBALL PITCH

You can't see my football pitch,
My football pitch is underground.
I can get free drinks and food,
Plus I can see good football matches,
I also get to meet the players,
But the best thing of all is that
No one knows about it, until now.

*Adam Macgill  (9)*
*Chopwell Primary School*


## SPEEDWAY

I love speedway,
It's really fun,
It's really dangerous
And watching it is fun.

The best teams in the league
Are really fun to watch,
But it's not really fun,
When your team loses the match!

*David P Murray  (9)*
*Chopwell Primary School*


## THE SUN BLAZE

A red hot star blazing through the clouds
That puts light on Earth that is there
For ever and ever.

*Georgia Hastie  (8)*
*Clover Hill Community Primary School*

## ALPHABET

A is for apple sweet and juicy.
B is for bells shiny and rustly.
C is for Cadbury's Crème Egg – yummy and creamy.
D is for dog, barking like bonkers.
E is for eagle, fluffy and sweet.
F is for frog, how he bounces and hops.
G is for grasshopper, noisy and spoilt.
H is for horse, big and strong.
I is for ice cream, cold and soft.
J is for jelly, wobbly and red.
K is for kitten, cute and small.
L is for chocolate log, flaky and delicious.
M is for money, shiny and round.
N is for night, dark and spooky.
O is for octopus, slimy and purple.
P is for penguin, who swims all day.
Q is for queen, good and big.
R is for rainbow, bright and colourful.
S is for snake, slimy and long.
T is for tiger, tall and strong.
U is for unicorn, big and white.
V is for vulture, hairy and noisy.
W is for walrus, slimy and fussy.
X is for Xmas, short word for Christmas.
Y is for yellow, a colour of the rainbow.
Z is for zebra, stripy and black.

*Jaynie Brooks  (8)*
*Clover Hill Community Primary School*

## ANIMAL ALPHABET ANTHOLOGY

A is for alligator, snappy, snap, snap,
B is for beaver, building his dam,
C is for cat, chasing the mouse,
D is for dog, who chased the cat,
E is for elephant, huge,
F is for flamingo, large and pink,
G is for gorilla, big and hairy,
H is for hyena, ha, ha, ha,
I is for iguana, I'm a reptile,
J is for jaguar, run, run, run,
K is for koala, climbing up a tree,
L is for lizard, very sneaky,
M is for mole, digging his hole,
N is for newt, hiding in the water,
O is for octopus, I've got eight legs,
P is for penguin, waddle, waddle, waddle,
Q is for quail, fluttering in the sky,
R is for reptile, crawling on the ground,
S is for snake, slithering on the ground,
T is for tortoise, I'm so slow,
Utterly brilliant, all these animals are,
V is for vixen, hunting her prey,
W is for worm, I'm slimy,
X is for x-ray fish, with a black and white pattern,
Y is for yak, shaggy and large,
Z is for zebra, very stripy.

*Sam Swinhoe  (9)*
*Clover Hill Community Primary School*

## MULTI BIRDS

Amazing
Birds,
Circle,
Dimension to dimension it's unbelievable.
Eagle,
Fieldfare,
Greenfinch,
Herring gull,
It's fantastic, isn't it?
Jays,
Kingfishers,
Long-tailed tits,
Magpie
Normal pied
Osprey,
Penguin,
Quail,
Raven black,
Swallow,
Thrush,
Vulture black,
White,
X-ray eyes,
Yellowhammer,
Zebra finch.

*David Hynman  (8)*
*Clover Hill Community Primary School*


## I WANT TO BE A STAR

I want to be a star,
With a really flash car.
I'd live in Hollywood,
If only I could!

People would stop me and stare
And take photos of me everywhere,
But then again, is it so good,
This living in Hollywood?

*Stephanie Longstaff  (10)*
*Clover Hill Community Primary School*


## UNDESERTED DINNER

My beans are            gnomes running for cover.

The sprouts are         the bushes where the gnomes are hiding.

This mashed potato is   a volcano flowing with lava.

My carrots are          logs burning to a crisp.

My knife is             a magic wand turning lava into water.

The jacket potato is a boat sailing upstream.

I have finished my dinner and the boat sinks.

*Ashlee Callaghan  (10)*
*Clover Hill Community Primary School*


## TABLE-TOP DINNER POEM

Cauliflower is like clouds in the sky,
Sprouts are swinging in the wind,
Carrots getting a suntan in the sun,
Cabbage swaying from side to side, like grass,
The leaves on the broccoli are rustling with the cabbage,
Mashed potato sheltering the animals.

*Christopher Hillcox  (9)*
*Clover Hill Community Primary School*

## UNDERWATER TABLE-TOP POEM

My pen is a torpedo, shot from a submarine,
The top of the table is the sandy bed of the ocean,
This piece of paper is the bottom of a cruise ship sailing overhead,
My eraser is a rock under which the crabs live.
These tiny bits left by the eraser are a shoal of fish darting by,
The little bits clustered round the pen are divers searching
for wrecks.
The pen is empty, we're running out of oxygen.
I'm gong to throw my pen away and clean my desk.
We are sailing back home, exhausted.

*Emma Stapleton  (10)*
*Clover Hill Community Primary School*


## LADYBIRD, LADYBIRD

Ladybird, ladybird, fly away home,
Night is approaching
And sunset has come,
So ladybird, ladybird, fly away quick.
Ladybird, ladybird, fly away home,
It's cold outside
And all the insects are gone.
Ladybird, ladybird fly away quick.

*Sophie Cox  (8)*
*Clover Hill Community Primary School*


## VAMPIRE BLUES

I haven't had an eyeball in ages,
I haven't had a neck to drink!
My mum's left the graveyard
And my dad's on a trip down the sink.

My fridge is quite empty,
My stomach is too,
But I've got an idea,
I'll just eat . . . you!

*Lucy Zwolinska  (8)*
*Clover Hill Community Primary School*


## RAINBOW

R   is for a red rose that grows in a garden,
A   is for anemones, all pretty colours,
I    is for ivy that grows up a house,
N   is for nettles that sting,
B   is for buttercups that shine in the sun,
O   is for orchids standing tall,
W   is for willow, swaying in the breeze.

*Sanchia Andries  (10)*
*Clover Hill Community Primary School*


## WHAT IS A GAME OF FOOTBALL?

Football is sport,
Football is scoring goals,
Football is tackling the opposite team,
Football is chasing the ball,
Football is saving goals,
Football is working as a team,
Football is a referee's whistle,
Football is watching The Premiership.

*Shaun Batey  (8)*
*Clover Hill Community Primary School*

## MOBY DICK

The big whale surfs along the sea,
He killed a boy named Lee.
Moby Dick eliminates little waves,
He can go through three caves.
Normal people can stand little waves.

Moby Dick fights against the Loch Ness monster,
This whale's bigger than a twelve foot lobster.
His last name's Dick and he cannot carry an ice pick.
Moby Dick won't fit in a swimming pool,
He can swim through a whale pool.

*Craig Ainscough (8)*
*Clover Hill Community Primary School*


## ITSY-BITSY SPIDER

Itsy-bitsy spider climbed up the water spout,
So I turned on the tap
And I washed the spider out.
But that dumb spider
Climbed up the spout again
And when he came in my bath tub,
I squashed him, what a pain!

*Amber Case (10)*
*Clover Hill Community Primary School*


## THE STAR

The
stars are
shimmering,
grey, sparkling
all the time.

A
star is
white
like snow and
glittery silver.

*Rachael Stillwell (8)*
*Clover Hill Community Primary School*


## FRIENDS

Tea for two
And two for tea,
I count on you
And you count on me.
I am your friend
And you are my friend too,
Together we will stay,
Forever as two.

*Nicola Brown (11)*
*Clover Hill Community Primary School*


## HARRY

Harry had a little sleep,
When he woke up he saw Bo-Peep.
Bo-Peep took him to see her sheep,
He looked down and saw something
He would like to keep.
Harry wanted Bo-Peep's sheep,
So that he could count them,
To help him get back to sleep!

*Leanne Butler (10)*
*Clover Hill Community Primary School*

## MY ROOM IS MESSY

My room is a mess.
Smelly socks, dirty dress,
Litter on the floor,
Posters on the door.
The only thing clean
Is my bed, where I rest my sleepy head.
My mum starts to scream,
My room is not clean!
I hope for the best, I hope for the best,
The only reason why
My room is a mess!

*Katy Martin (10)*
*Clover Hill Community Primary School*


## FLOWERS

F   lowers grow in all places,
L   ovely smells come into the air,
O   rchids and violets, tulips and snowdrops,
W   ater and air make us grow,
E   legantly attracting insects,
R   abbits eat us and our leaves,
S   hhh! It is now time to sleep.

*Craig Batey (10)*
*Clover Hill Community Primary School*


## ROLLER COASTER

I rode the roller coaster
It gave me such a scare
I'm sure I left some skid marks
In my underwear

When the ride was over
I scrambled from my seat
The last thing on my mind
Was having *more* to eat!

**James Knott  (10)**
**Clover Hill Community Primary School**


## GREYHOUND RACING

Pushing,
Shoving,
Everywhere,
Racing,
Passing,
With no care.
People shouting all around
For the fastest greyhound.
Look at my hound, he's the winner,
I know he'll eat his scrumptious dinner.

**Elicia Hills  (11)**
**Clover Hill Community Primary School**


## THE GHOUL

My friend lives beside a graveyard,
But at night,
He can hear leaves crunching beneath boots,
Doors squeaking, loud boots stamping on the stairs,
Large, muddy hands smudging against his door.

**Connor Butler  (8)**
**Clover Hill Community Primary School**

## The Train

The train storms through the countryside,
The wind is on its tail.
The people in its carriages
Are sheltered from the gale.

Lots of people talking
On their mobile phones,
The jangling in my ears,
The variety of tones.

*Alex Clapham  (10)*
*Clover Hill Community Primary School*


## Underworld Planet

The weeds are like bushes waving in the wind
The fish is like stars gleaming in the water
The shells are like counters in the classroom
The swordfish is like an eraser beginning to rub out
The shark is like a minotaur's bones charging to a man
The jellyfish is like a stone on the beach stamping on everything.

*Steven J Hall  (9)*
*Clover Hill Community Primary School*


## Table Top Madness

The tiny little bits left by the rubber are ants.
The brown table is soil where the ants live.
The ruler is a bridge where the ants scurry across.
The pencil sharpener is a car for the ants to travel about.

The pencil is a tall lamppost so the ants can find
their way home in the dark.
Suddenly the ants are swept into the bin
by one sweep of my hand.

*Alexander Edward Hewson  (9)*
*Clover Hill Community Primary School*


## WE WENT TO A FARM

We went to a farm,
The cows were calm,
Mooing all day long.
We hung up our coats,
To see the goats,
Which were inside the barn.

*Joshua Telfer  (11)*
*Clover Hill Community Primary School*


## COMETS

Comets are long shooting stars
That shoot through outer space
They look like a mini shining silvery sun
It is so super
People say it is like a big big superstar to them!

*Katrina Powell  (7)*
*Clover Hill Community Primary School*

## BEACH TABLE-TOP

My pen is a rather small person,
Sunbathing on the smooth sand.
The large table-top is vast golden beach.
The pencil pots are tall palm trees
Reaching to the sun.
This blue piece of paper is the sea swishing softly.
My eraser is a pillow,
Which my pen rests its tired head on.
These little bits left by the eraser
Are pretty shells with patterns on.
The little bits are clustered round the pen.
Some children have covered my man in shells as a joke.
My pen is empty. My man has an empty stomach
And wants something to eat.
I'm going to throw my pen away.
A strong wind carries him away,
Dropping him into a dirty pit.

*Heather Shaw  (10)*
*Clover Hill Community Primary School*


## PLUTO

Pluto is a big
Silver ball shining in the sky,
When I look at it, it makes me cry
'Oh my, oh my.' It is very old
and very cold . . .
But I still like it, don't you?

*Hannah Lovatt  (8)*
*Clover Hill Community Primary School*

## THE UNDERWATER WORLD

The pencil pot is a submarine
Submerging into the sea.
The pen is a harpoon gun
To fire a squirming shark.
The red lead is the blood of the
Dying great white shark.
The green pencil is the slimy seaweed
At the bottom of the sea.
The tiny bits of rubber are
A school of sharks sensing
The shark's blood.
The pen is empty.
I've got to tidy up.
Now the divers have packed up
And re-emerged to the surface.

*Michael Haig  (9)*
*Clover Hill Community Primary School*

## TOTAL ECLIPSE

A silver circle covering the sun
It's sparkling, floating in mid air.
It's making the sun very dark.

The bright sun
Bringing light to all
When suddenly
It goes very dark
It's called a total eclipse.

*Jennifer Mutch  (8)*
*Clover Hill Community Primary School*

## MY TERRORS OF THE DEEP POEM

My pen is a spiky swordfish searching for little fish.
The top of the table is the deep blue sea.
This piece of paper is a flat fish swimming in the depths.
My rubber is an oil rig with divers searching for oil.
My pencil case is an orca chasing an innocent seal.
My book is a jellyfish washed up on the shore.
The ruler is a great white shark desperate for human flesh.
The pen is empty. The swordfish is hungry, he needs food.
I'm going to throw the pen away.
The orca catches the swordfish and swallows him whole.
I'm going to clean my desk out
*Bang* the oil rig blows up and the sea life is no longer.

*Tony McMeiken  (10)*
*Clover Hill Community Primary School*


## THE MONSTER WORLD

The pencil pot is a dark, gloomy cave.
The yellow sandpaper is the sandy ground.
Little scrunched up tissues are the big grey rocks.
My pencils are the tall trees.
The blue books are the soft calm sea.
Different colours of lead are large ugly monsters.
The little pieces of rubber are the slimy fish
For the monsters' bait.
A ping-pong ball is an asteroid which had
Destroyed the monsters' world
And the monsters have died.

*Lee Goldsbrough  (10)*
*Clover Hill Community Primary School*

## WINTER TABLETOP POEM

My pen is a frozen tree trunk lying all alone.

The top of the table is an ice rink never been skated on.

This piece of paper is freshly fallen white snow.

My eraser is the dull colourless sun asleep in the sky.

These tiny bits left by the eraser are the melting drips of ice.

The little bits clustered round the pen is
Soggy grey slush clinging to the tree trunk.

The pen is empty. The hollow tree trunk
provides shelter from the cold for animals.

I'm going to throw my pen away and clean my desk.
The tree trunk is collected and thrown into the fire for fuel.

The animals have no home.

*Danielle Armstrong  (9)*
*Clover Hill Community Primary School*


## TABLE-TOP SEA

My pen is a submarine submerging under water.
My paper is the bottom of the sea which we sink to,
To find the remains of a ship.
My rubber is a boat on the surface of the water.
My ruler is a whale emerging right at me.
I swerve to miss it.
My sharpener is a rock that I hit after swerving the whale.

*Jason Bell  (10)*
*Clover Hill Community Primary School*

# A POEM UNDER THE SEA

The table top is the sandy floor.

The pens are tall towering rocks
In which fish hide.

The pieces of paper are treasure maps
dropped by the pirates sitting above.

My rubber is an anchor dropped down
from a pirate ship above
while they look for the lost maps.

The tiny bits left by the rubber
are the fish swimming frantically
away from the chasing shark.

The rulers are the sharks chasing the fish.

The little bits are clustered round the pen.
They want to hide and be safe from the sharks.

The desk is cleaned and my things are put away.
The fish are swept away by the falling cascade of rocks.

*Amy Gray (10)*
*Clover Hill Community Primary School*


# THE LONELY SHOOTING STAR

The lonely shooting star
Glides through space.
Space is in the creepy darkness.
The star is very scarlet.

*Jayne Drummond (7)*
*Clover Hill Community Primary School*

## TABLETOP RACE TRACK POEM

My table is                          a race track, big and wide.

These rulers are                     barriers for cars to bash into.

My rubber is                         the starting block where the race begins.

The bits from
the rubber are                       people standing cheering.

My pencil case is                    a racing car speeding around the track.

My pen top is                        a box for the commentator to stand on.

I'm going to pack
everything away now.                 The race is over until next year.

*Jamie Barclay  (9)*
*Clover Hill Community Primary School*

## TABLE TO - A PERSON'S FACE

The two pencil sharpeners are dazzling like diamonds,
The pen is a long fat nose sniffing the air.
The paper is a pale white face.
The ruler is a long thick mouth.
The books are two big floppy ears
Listening to the thump thump of a giant
Earthling coming to wipe the desk.
It's coming closer, it's coming closer, *bang!*

Now all that is left is a little line of pen
Where the pen was.

*Lucy Sage  (9)*
*Clover Hill Community Primary School*

## TABLE TOP DEEP BLUE SEA

The top of the table is the soft beige sand,
Under the table is the swishing blue sea,
My pen is a spinning dolphin jumping
In and out of the deep clear water,
My eraser is a chest full of fish, gold and silver.
The bits left off my eraser are baby shrimps
Swimming by the seaweed,
My paper is a stingray blending in
With the soft soggy sand,
My pen is tired so it stops for some sleep
On the bottom of the blue ocean,
I am going to throw my pen away
And clean my desk,
The dolphin finds a friend and vanishes
To another place.

*Melissa Appleby  (10)*
*Clover Hill Community Primary School*


## THE FLYING PEN

The flying pen is a clever pen,
It flies all over the Earth.
If you look at it closely
You can see little aliens.
The pen can fly all over Mars as well.
It came back but the teacher told me off.
I had an idea the pen was magic.
I said abracadabra and there was
Writing and the teacher was big eyed!

*Craig M Green  (9)*
*Clover Hill Community Primary School*

## TABLE TOP TRAGEDY

| | |
|---|---|
| My pen is | a skateboarder, whizzing round the table. |
| My rubber is | a skateboard ready to be stood on. |
| The table is | the skate park full of ramps. |
| The piece of paper is | the entrance to the skate park. |
| The bits clustered round the pen are | leaves getting blown round by the wind. |
| The pen is empty. | The man has fallen and crashed. |
| I'm going to throw my pen away and clean my desk. | The man no longer lives and the park has been swept. |

*Thomas Oliver Morrison  (10)*
*Clover Hill Community Primary School*


## TABLE TOP WINTER

My pen is a frozen river.

The top of the table is a field full of snow.

My rubber is a sledge speeding down a hill.

These tiny bits clustered around the pen
are children happily building a snowman.

The empty pen is a river slowly melting into water.

I am going to throw my pen away and clear my desk.
The river dries up in the hot summer sunshine.

*Danielle Cromarty  (9)*
*Clover Hill Community Primary School*

## GHOSTS HAUNTING

G hosts and ghouls in the haunted house,
H aunting very loudly but, as quiet as a mouse,
'O oooooooh,' wails the ghost,
S weeping through post,
T orturing the other ghosts with his noise,
S weeping through, especially the boys.

'H a, ha, ha,' the ghosts call,
A rching round to the wall,
U sing people's souls as food,
N ot caring about their moods.
T easing other ghosts like hell,
I gnoring others, very well.
N aughty, wrecking furniture lots,
G oing into the garden pots.

*Sophie Delarny (8)*
*Clover Hill Community Primary School*


## A FARMER'S YARD

The farmer's yard works all day
Never stops to get the bay.
The mash on my plate is
the field the farmer ploughs.
When it is straight he gets the beans
and spreads them into the soil.
The hay he gives to the animals
is my delicious spaghetti.
The bushes are as green as my sprouts.
As a human comes to eat
there is no food on the plate.

*Harvey Willis (10)*
*Clover Hill Community Primary School*

## GHOSTLY GHOUL

The ghosts fly around the room,
Then crashing, giving a boom.
An ugly ghost roars
And scares everyone out the doors.
The ghost flies out the door,
Then making a big roar,
A comet flies down to Earth,
When baby's having its birth.
The ghost pinches a small sword,
Then goes and slices a cord.
Then getting a witch's spell book,
He says the magic words - hook, book, took.
Then leaving everyone's houses a mess,
He departs and gives everyone a bless.

*Michael Brown  (8)*
*Clover Hill Community Primary School*




## MY TEAM

L   iverpool are the best team ever,
I   n other people's opinions they sure will tremor.
V   ile teams we surely will thrash,
E   nding in fans with lots of trash.
R   iise goes in defence, midfield,
P   enalties in the Charity Shield,
O   wen beats the defence with pace,
O   ver the keeper, he chips the ball with grace.
L   iverpool Football Club are ace.

*James Farrey  (10)*
*Clover Hill Community Primary School*

## MOUNTAIN

In the summer, when you wake up
From your misty dreams,
You find yourself on a mountain top,
Well at least, that's what it seems.
You're still in your pyjamas and
You're as cold as a block of ice,
When a man walks up behind you and says,
'Please roll the dice.'
You wonder what he means,
But still you roll the dice on your bed.
'Goodbye,' the man says.
You close your eyes, then open them,
You're back in your warm room.
You look down at your bed and there lies . . .
The dice!

*Bethany Walker  (9)*
*Clover Hill Community Primary School*


## CRAIG, THE CROCODILE

Craig, the crocodile, goes 'snap, snap, snap!'
Dentists beware, it's a trap.
Likes to eat,
Meat is a treat.
Think he is sleeping,
He will be peeping and waiting for you.
Likes to crunch bones,
Those teeth can crack stones.
Those green, lumpy scales
Are smaller than whales.

*Michael Richardson  (8)*
*Clover Hill Community Primary School*

## ANIMALS

*Dolphins*

Someone said long ago
Dolphins guided ships to shore.
They swim all day,
Peacefully as can be,
Playing in the ice-cold water with their friends.

*Dog*

Wakes in the morning
From being asleep,
Gets an ice-cold drink.
It begs for its food,
It goes outside and chases cats
And has fun all day.

***Serena Pacitti  (8)***
***Clover Hill Community Primary School***


## TABLE TOP POEM

My rubber is lots of teeny weeny ants scurrying to their home.

My paper is a plank of wood disguising their home.

My sharpener is a combine harvester working in the fields.

My pencil is a farmer with big black wellies on
stamping on all the little ants.

I'm going to clean my desk away now.
The farmer picks up the plank of wood and throws it away.

***Emma Smith  (9)***
***Clover Hill Community Primary School***

## WHIRLWIND

The wind is coming out today,
Sweeping up a few cards to play.
The wind is coming out today,
Yes, the wind is coming out today.
The wind is coming out today,
Brushing out a house today.
The wind is coming out today,
Gliding past a little girl called Kay.
The wind is coming out today,
The wind is coming your way.
The wind is coming very fast,
Beware, you never know, it might come past.
You!

*Michaela Forbes (8)*
*Clover Hill Community Primary School*


## A STRIPY ZEBRA

S   is for a shiny, short coat,
T   is for a tail swishing by,
R   is for roving across the grass,
I    is for always being intelligent,
P   is for prancing about,
Y   is for young ones with their mums.

Z   is for zebra in a herd,
E   is for eating all together,
B   is for being brave,
R   is for running from danger,
A   is for a zebra who eats apples.

*Chelsey Mason (9)*
*Clover Hill Community Primary School*

## A POEM OF NESSIE THE MONSTER

I am a strange dinosaur,
I live in a lake.
I eat seaweed and plants,
But beware, do not go in the lake,
Or I'll gobble you up.
I have no friends
Because I ate them last night.
You have been warned,
I'm not finished yet.
Some people have seen me,
That is not true,
But I would like some fun.
You may think if I'm a dinosaur
I would have gone,
But no, I stayed.

*Carter Rippon (9)*
*Clover Hill Community Primary School*


## MY BROTHER

M   y brother is seven years old,
Y   es! We're always fighting, if asked.
B   rown hair is what he has,
R   ight! He's a little, cheeky monkey.
O   ther thing that bothers me is . . .
T   orturing all the time.
H   e's a really kind boy at heart.
E   nemy – he is sometimes to me.
R   emember, he's still only young.

*Kathryn Craig (9)*
*Clover Hill Community Primary School*

## A HEALTHY SCHOOL

A  healthy school is a happy school.

H  ealthy temptation is the best rule,
E  ating all the good things, but sometimes letting go,
A  lways trying to let being healthy flow.
L  ifestyle is important,
T  ropical fruit and blackcurrant,
H  aving plenty of food, but keeping healthy too,
Y  uk to drugs, smoke and drink, is what you do.

S  ipping water all day long,
C  arrots, not crisps, will keep you strong.
H  obbies outside will keep you fit,
O  pen spaces in which to sit.
O  outside life is here to stay,
L  iving healthily is nature's way.

*Jamie Leech (10)*
*Clover Hill Community Primary School*


## UNDERWATER TABLE-TOP POEM

My pen is a submarine abandoned years ago.
The table top is the deep blue ocean stretching far and wide.
My rubber is a huge blue whale, hunting for its prey.
The tiny bits left by the rubber are tropical fish,
Dodging the whale's jaws.
This piece of paper in a deserted island,
Left by its inhabitants many years ago.
The pencil pot is a large, sturdy mountain
With its sea anemones clinging to its sides.
I clear my desk, the whale has eaten all the fish.

*John Richardson (10)*
*Clover Hill Community Primary School*

## SATURN

Saturn is round
It is bright.
Saturn is white
Orange and yellow
Shines in space.
Saturn zooms so
Fast and smoothly.
It is in space
For life and
For many more
Years
Too.

*Scott Swinhoe  (8)*
*Clover Hill Community Primary School*

## A ROCKET

A
rocket
that can
fly high
into space.
Lots of white
and grey smoke
comes out from
the rocket. It's
like a mist on
the ground. You
might not see it again.

*Miriam Atkinson  (7)*
*Clover Hill Community Primary School*

# A ROCKET

A rocket
zooms far
into space past
the sparkling
stars with
smiles on
their face.
Ahead they
see planet Mars
then land on it
with a
*Bang!*

*Kathryn Tinson  (7)*
*Clover Hill Community Primary School*


# THE LOVELY SHINING SUN

The sun is a big star
And lies in space.
I'm in space and I'm very hot.

*Monique Kelsey  (7)*
*Clover Hill Community Primary School*


# METEORITES

Huge shiny rock -
Solid flaming meteorites
Speeding past rockets.

*Peter Robson  (8)*
*Clover Hill Community Primary School*

# THE SUN

A big flaming fireball
floating everywhere in space.
It's a giant, flying, shining star.
It gives heat to other planets
And shining galaxies.

*Aaron Wilson  (7)*
*Clover Hill Community Primary School*


# THE MOON

The moon is cold.
The moon is very white.
When you look up you will see it.
The moon is bright.

*Serena Sahota  (8)*
*Clover Hill Community Primary School*


# THE COMET

A red and yellow comet
Is a beautiful shooting star
Which flies around in space.
It's bright, fast and colourful.
I'd like to see it race.

*Catriona Bathan  (8)*
*Clover Hill Community Primary School*

## SHOOTING STARS

Stars
shooting
across space, shining in the
glittering night. The
shooting stars
pass the
hot sun
and all the
other planets.

*Hannah McColl (7)*
*Clover Hill Community Primary School*


## MONKEY

We watched the monkeys in the zoo,
I think the monkeys watched us too,
With big, sad eyes, they seemed to say,
'Could we swap places for just one day?'

*Mark Ainsley (11)*
*Clover Hill Community Primary School*


## THE SUN

The sun is a flaming scarlet star,
It has got shining hot heat
And the heat travels to Earth.
The sun is a hot ball of gas,
If an astronaut travelled there
They would have died.

*Hannah Whyte (7)*
*Clover Hill Community Primary School*

## DOG FOOD PIE

We all thought my grannie could see,
For she's never needed glasses.
We all found out one Thursday night,
When she made me - dog food pie!

It all happened one peaceful night,
When she made one big pie.
She poured dog food into the pastry -
Bless her, she thought it was mince.

I waited one hour and twenty minutes,
Patient and silent, and then,
When I finally got to eat it,
I cried out loud, 'What's this?'

Now my grannie wears glasses,
I suppose it's for her own good.
At least I won't be counting on having
Any more pie surprises!

*Jessica Turner (11)*
*Clover Hill Community Primary School*


## DEEP IN THE JUNGLE

King of the jungle,
Dozing, sleeping, lazing in the sun.
Sharp claws and pointed teeth,
Long, thin, swishy tail all day.
The lion roaring in the sun,
All of the jungle hears the lion roar.
The lion eats its enemies all up.

*Louise Morrod (9)*
*Clover Hill Community Primary School*

## THE PENGUIN

The penguin waddles along in the snow
With its stiff legs (so it is slow).
Swishing and struggling to get to the sea,
Hoping to catch some fish for tea.

When it's time to play,
He swims fast, sometimes catching prey.
Crashing and splashing in the ocean,
Darting through in fast motion.

At night he meets his family,
His mum, his dad and his brother, Stanley.
Then it's time to eat some fish,
Enjoying the juicy, scrumptious dish.

*Matthew Bracchi  (9)*
*Clover Hill Community Primary School*

## THE SUN

The sun is a glowing worm that gives you a sunburn.
The sun is like an egg yolk, all yellow and messy.
Yellow buttercups in the field picked three by three,
Yellow corn ready to be picked by the farmer soon.
Then the sun says, 'I have got lots of friends,
The moon, Mars, Pluto, Neptune.'
In the morning, the sun rises at 5am and
Stays there all day until it goes down.
Some people say that you should not look at the sun
Because it is very bright.

*Jennifer Brown  (9)*
*Clover Hill Community Primary School*

## BROTHERS

B rothers,
R ough as can be,
O h I am sick of them!
T hey are cute half the time,
H orrible most of the time,
E ither hitting me or making fun of me,
R unning around like lunatics!
S ometimes I feel sorry for them,
   I said *sometimes!*

*Jordan Hewitt (9)*
*Clover Hill Community Primary School*


## ASTRONOMY

Astronomy is an amazing bright colourful thing
Up in the dark misty sky,
Along with the shiny stars
Have a look you might catch
A glimpse of astronomy.

*Ross Pembroke (8)*
*Clover Hill Community Primary School*


## FUNFAIR

I scream and scream on the funfair wheel,
I giggle in the mirror room,
I panic on the ghost train,
I shout on the waltzer, 'Let me off!'
I love to eat the candyfloss and try my luck on the games,
But my favourite of them all is the roller-coaster.

*Casey Graham (10)*
*Cragside Primary School*

# MY SECRET GARDEN

I have a secret garden, I call it 'Angel Row,'
It's the prettiest place I've ever seen and it's where my flowers grow.

It has got its own gazebo where the children sit and play,
Or they can shelter from the cold on a wet and windy day.

It also has a little pond, filled with plants and fish.
In the corner is a miniature well, where you can make a wish.

You can pick out lots of colours in the flowers and the shrubs,
Pink and yellow, blue and green, together in the tubs.

The lawn is neat and tidy, the gardener keeps it so,
With all his tools upon the shelf and the water hose down below.

A little statue of a boy stands there against the wall,
It's actually a fountain though, with a tiny waterfall.

There are many trees in my garden, such as apple, cherry and pear,
They attract a lot of different birds who watch and stand and stare.

There's also a wooden bird box and the birds fly in and out,
Trying hard to make a nest with the things which are lying about.

There are twigs and grass, straw and leaves and often bits of hay,
The children love to watch them and feed them every day.

A wooden bench has been made to sit out on sunny days,
The old people can enjoy the view and talk about the olden days.

There's room to have a picnic on the grass when it is fine,
You can look at the beautiful flowers, while enjoying
The warm sunshine.

When I look at my secret garden, it makes me very glad,
It's so pretty, pleasant and colourful, the best birthday present
I've had.

*Ashleigh Collins (11)*
*Cragside Primary School*


## THE FUNNY TALE

Once upon a hill,
There was a girl called Jill.
Her brother was a maniac,
Their mother was ill.

Their neighbour had a lot of cows,
We thought he was quite barmy,
He lived in a little house
And his name was Marny.

Their father ran away one day
And was never seen again,
We thought he was hiding in the hay,
But we found him in our den.

Now we're coming to the end,
There's not much else to say,
I've told the story, now it's goodbye,
I'll see you another day.

*Nikki Anderson (10)*
*Cragside Primary School*

## HIDDEN TREASURE

Hidden treasure sitting there,
Right in front of my greedy stare.

The thought of silver, gold and jewels
Makes the greedy hunter drool.

The sweaty palms, the clinging vest,
The heave digging has left him out of breath.

The sandy shores, the salty sea,
These riches that now belong to me.

He lifts the lid of the wooden chest,
He prays that he has been truly blessed.

The hinges howl
Like a pack of hungry wolves.

The treasure is here,
Glory is near.

His face lights up like a sparkle in the sun,
He lifts the chest up, 'Oh what a ton.'

The boat sways to and fro,
He hopes to get home before the sun goes.

He opens the door to his shabby old home,
His rickety old chair will soon be a throne.

*Daniel Holmes  (11)*
*Cragside Primary School*


## THE JOURNEY

Me and my dad went out in his car,
We went on a journey that was ever so far.
We went in the country, where nobody goes,
Where the trees sway and stand in a row.

Then my dad says its time to go home,
When I get home he says goodbye.
My eye sees him out of sight
When the lights are so bright.

*Martin Hall  (11)*
*Cragside Primary School*


## A MAN IN JUNE

I once saw
A man in June
Sitting on a garden bench.

He said to me,
'Have you seen
the dragon in my garden pond?'

I said 'No,'
He said, 'Go
And see it for yourself.'

He pointed left,
I went right,
But there was no pond in my sight.

I turned round
And saw on the ground
A puddle I'd walked right through,

And there on the floor,
Beside the door,
Was a dragonfly, floating in a misty haze.

*Thomas Foy  (11)*
*Cragside Primary School*

# FIGHTING WITH THE MOON

Rippling waves of sapphire blue,
Lapping at the lazy shore,
Welcoming in the sunshine rays
And softly calling out for more.

Washing round the jagged rocks,
Searching out the bay,
Dragging up the seaweed
And anything in its way.

The nights grow cold
And the waves turn grey,
And the sea decreases
To a gentle sway.

Then the waves got rougher
And the icy rain did pour.
The sea cries out in anger
As it argues with the shore,

And then the ocean's rival appears,
Like a distant silver balloon.
The sea is roaring, battling,
Fighting with the moon.

*Emma Humphries (10)*
*Cragside Primary School*


## CANDY, THE CAT AND BEN, THE DOG

Playing in the garden, scratching in the house,
Candy pounces to catch a mouse.
Sniffing all around, waiting for some food,
Ben sleeps, he is not in the playing mood.

Ben wakes up and does not make a sound
As Candy looks at him thinking, what a smelly hound.
They both start to play and it ends up in a fight,
They are both hurt, it serves them right.

*Victoria Canham  (11)*
*Cragside Primary School*


## MY FIELD OF DEATH

I saw them,
They walked in my field,
Saw them I did with my blood-red eyes,
Evil in my heart lies.

All who have dared to challenge my powers
Have lain lifeless in my field for eternity.
Don't cross this line,
You'll be far from fine.

I came out from where I hide
To catch those who disturb my pride.
Behind them I crept,
My black hands on their shoulders I kept,
To dust slowly they turned.

Turning away to my hands, I looked,
Defeat me no one could,
Tried they did,
Defeat me no one could.

I laughed and laughed,
Defeat me no one could.
Cross this line and you will see,
For no one can defeat me!

*Roszeen Afsar  (10)*
*Cragside Primary School*

## AMBER, THE DOG

Open the front door
And she's off downstairs towards me,
Here come the licks,
Now I'm soaked.
Oh, now I'm being jumped on,
In go her razor-sharp claws,
And we're on the floor.
My packed lunch is getting the make-over now,
And I flop down on the settee,
But ouch, she's after my zip.
That's another zip ruined.
Time for tea and she's sticking her nose in my chest,
Scrounging away.
Bath time now, hardly enough time to shut the door,
Before she's in, drinking the bath water.
Bedtime and I'm tossing and turning, because she's in the bin.
Oh Amber, what a nuisance!

*Heather Buchan  (10)*
*Cragside Primary School*


## UNTITLED

The palm trees waved
As I looked at my map
And the sand glittered
As I pulled down my cap.

There it was in front of me,
A wooden chest,
Full of gold and silver
And the rest.

I opened the chest with my key
To see sapphires, emeralds,
Diamonds and pearls,
Gold and silver coins all sparkling at me.

The palm trees waved
As I put away my map
And the sand glittered
As I pulled up my cap.

*Emma Jobson  (11)*
*Cragside Primary School*


## HIDDEN TREASURE

The sparkling sun above the sea,
I see the treasure beneath me.
I've searched and searched for many years
And there it is with the dancing bears.

They all look down to the golden chest,
To dive down deep would be a test.
I open it and to my surprise,
I see jewels before my eyes, glittering slightly, all of a size.

Golden coins are ten a penny,
Rubies red, there are many.
All they need is my polish clean
To make the emeralds glittering green.

I think something's running through my mind,
Telling me to be kind.
I'll share and share, because that's who I am,
I'm Tich, the very magical man!

*Leanne Bower  (10)*
*Cragside Primary School*

## HIDDEN TREASURE

I've found the hidden treasure,
Oh so precious to me,
More precious than the diamonds
That glisten so brightly.

Now sometimes they embarrass you,
We argue with them too,
But sometimes I underestimate
How much they mean to me.

I love these people very much,
We get along happily,
For the people I care for so dearly,
Are my family!

*Alexandra Sinton  (10)*
*Cragside Primary School*


## COLOUR GIRL

Red is the colour of fire,
Silver is the colour of wire,
Yellow is the colour of a lemon,
Green is the colour of a melon,
Orange is the colour of the sun,
Purple is the colour of a plum,
Blue is the colour of the sea,
Brown is the colour of a tree,
Gold is the colour of a ring,
White is the colour of a wing.

*Jane Potts  (11)*
*Cragside Primary School*

## HIDDEN TREASURE

Hidden treasure beneath the sea,
Who will find it, you or me?
Hidden treasure on the land,
Who will have it in their hand?
Gold or rubies, what will it be?
Whatever it is, I hope who finds it is me.
Maybe it's love or friendship too,
There is more in the world than just me and you.
It could be diamonds or rocks so bright,
Whatever it is, it might give you a fright.
But maybe it's nothing, just a message from He,
He who made the world and most of all . . .
You and me!

*Lisa Hardy  (11)*
*Cragside Primary School*

## HIDDEN TREASURES

It's a quest to find the treasure.
If I found it, it would be a great pleasure.

It could be deep in the sea,
Waiting for you or me.

Or it could be on the land,
Deep in the red-hot sand.

Maybe it's in the sky,
Near the things that fly,

But what if someone has got it,
And that person is I?

*Andrew Wilkinson  (10)*
*Cragside Primary School*

## HIDDEN TREASURE

After searching the globe
For many years,
There it lies
Beneath my eyes.

The diamond saliva
Running from the chest's mouth
And the golden tongue,
Licking me as I stroke it.

I never knew
Who would eventually find it,
But now I know,
Because it lives with me.

*Michael Keen  (11)*
*Cragside Primary School*


## HIDDEN TREASURES

I was swimming in the sea at my leisure,
When I came across some hidden treasure,
So down at the bottom of the deep blue sea,
I've got a secret for you and me.

There's lots of gold and diamond rings
And lots and lots of other things.
There were pearls and emeralds and rubies too,
Lots of goodies for me and you.

So when you go to the bottom of the sea,
Remember the treasure belongs to *me*.

*Sammy Bertram  (11)*
*Cragside Primary School*

## LIVERPOOL, THE REDS

Liverpool Football Club are the best,
From north to south
And east to west.
They have excellent players,
That's why I'm a fan,
Like Heskey, Redknapp, Murphy and Hamman.

Owen and Gerrard are Scousers through and through,
And they could score ten goals against Man U.

The Reds are the greatest in the land,
And they play at Anfield, with the famous Cop stand.

*Shaun Douglas  (11)*
*Cragside Primary School*

## HIDDEN TREASURE

On an island, as quiet as could be,
There it was in front of me.
The palm trees waving as if to say,
'You've found it, you've found it. Hip, hip, hooray.'
There it was, the golden hair,
As the sun was heating the air.
Sapphire cyes sparkling like the sea,
Ruby lips as red as could be.
Gold, rubies, sapphires are precious to me,
But not as precious as my sister could be.

*Louise Hutchinson  (11)*
*Cragside Primary School*

# HIDDEN TREASURE

Deep, deep
Beneath the sea,
A hidden treasure
Was waiting for me.

Many had tried
To get that chest,
Guarded by what
I call a pest.

The chest is wooden
And very old
And has a few bits
On the side, which are gold.

Inside, it has
Treasures galore,
Which pirates had stolen
Years ago.

Like gold and silver,
Fit for a king,
With that
You could buy anything.

But now someone's found it
And taken it home.
That person is me
And that's the end of my poem.

*Louise Parr (11)*
*Cragside Primary School*

## HIDDEN TREASURE

I went in search of treasure one day
On board a pirate ship.
We sailed to Madagascar,
And on to Reykjavik.

We dreamed of gold, sapphires and rubies,
But all we saw was a
Chest full of jam,
Guarded by a clam.

We sailed for home
Without any treasure,
When we saw our families,
Oh what a pleasure!

*Martin Anderson  (10)*
*Cragside Primary School*

## JOURNEYS

J   umping up, turning round,
O   ver the hill, on the ground,
U   p the road, over the hedge,
R   ound the cliff on the edge,
N   umb fingers, numb toes,
E   xactly where I'm going, nobody knows.
Y   ou're going on a journey,
S   uddenly, your tummy goes churny.

*Dan Scott  (11)*
*Cragside Primary School*

## THE FIRE

Raging red flames grab trees like snakes,
Roaring like tigers, you grow larger and larger,
Your thick black smoke swirls all around,
Only water can stamp you out,
Then you will be calm again.

*Leanne Kennedy  (11)*
*Cragside Primary School*


## HIDDEN TREASURE

There was some treasure in a wood,
Hidden in a tree.
Lots of gold is good,
Especially for me.

*Stephen Watson  (8)*
*Hawthorn Primary School*


## COOL BREEZE

As I watch the birds go by,
I stand in the breeze and wait a while.
I see the squirrels skip along
As the cool breeze blows their fur.

I watch all the creatures hop by
As my heart feels warmer than ever.
I sing a tune to go with this
And this I know will not escape from my heart,
And you also know that your heart is warm.

*Sarah Horne  (10)*
*Ivy Road Primary School*

## SUMMER

The sun,
The sand,
The shade from the tree,
The buzzing from the bumblebee.

The morning,
The night,
Both so bright,
Sun shining through till I'm tucked up tight.

The flowers,
The birds,
The butterfly flirts,
Fluttering round in quick little spurts.

The six weeks break from school we get,
Summer's my favourite season,
And yours, I bet.

*Sarah Husband (10)*
*Ivy Road Primary School*


## ON A HOT SUMMER'S DAY

On a hot summer's day,
My friends and I went out to play.
We hopped and scotched and jumped around,
We went to the lake where ducks we found.
We broke up bread to feed the ducks
Then  watched fishermen put worms on their hooks.
We toddled off home to have some tea,
And told my mum of the things we'd been to see.

*Charlie O'Brien (10)*
*Ivy Road Primary School*

# MY FRIEND

Who plays all day without any fuss,
Who runs and runs without getting tired,
Who will always stay your very best friend
Even when you are in a huff?

Who always waits until you come from school,
Who jumps up and down and chases you around,
Who barks and howls to say hello,
Who licks you all over from head to toe?

Who helps to dry you after the bath,
Who eats the bubbles and makes you laugh,
Who chews your slippers and your favourite socks,
Who pinches your pencils and stuffed, furry fox?

Who never likes to wet his coat,
Who never takes a shower,
Who rolls around the carpet,
Having a mad half hour?

Who likes to walk in the rain or snow,
Who never wears any clothes,
Who always has a friend or two,
No matter where he goes?

Who sits up high on the kitchen chair,
Who likes a bone to chew,
Who always wants a taste of your tea,
Even if it's horrible stew!

Who is covered in fur from head to tail
And has a big, black nose,
Who finds me when we play hide-and-seek,
No matter where I go?

Have you guessed who my friend could be?
It's Jasper, the dog,
Who is so good to me.

*Andrew Jobling  (10)*
*Ivy Road Primary School*


## MY BROTHER DAN

Here is Dan who is the shape of a pan,
Here is Dan who has got a tan,
Here is Dan who walks like an old man,
Here is Dan who speaks like an old gran,
Here is Dan who has crinkles like an old man,
Here is Dan who got slapped by his mam,
Here is Dan who bought a fan,
Here is Dan who got told off by a policeman,
Here is Dan who smashed a full jar of jam,
Here is Dan who broke his glasses which used to be his gran's,
Here is Dan whose finger got chopped off by the fan,
Here is Dan whose knee was bleeding from a cut from a can,
Here is Dan who has got a walking stick like his gran,
Here is Dan who was hit on the head with a frying pan,
Here is Dan who got fried in the frying pan,
Here is Dan who ate five pieces of ham,
Here is Dan whose auntie is called Pam.

*Liam Dickson  (11)*
*Ivy Road Primary School*

## A Day At School

Running round all crazy,
Jumping high through hoops,
Skipping through a tunnel,
Hear the bell for school.

Learning in a lesson,
Got nothing to do,
But sit around and wait,
Until it's time to go.

Racing home for tea,
Who's gonna be at home?
Don't know what I'm having,
Want to have some fun
Before I go back to my bed
And snuggle up tight, warm.

*Hayley Cameron  (11)*
*Ivy Road Primary School*


## Dolphins, Dolphins

Smiling faces, friendly eyes,
Swimming together beneath the skies.

Leaping and frolicking into the sea,
What a wonderful life it must be.

Swimming and gliding, lots of fun,
What a beautiful sight for everyone.

Beautiful creatures, happy and gay,
My dream to swim with them will come true one day.

*Amy Scott  (10)*
*Ivy Road Primary School*

## APPLES

Apples, apples, crisp and green,
Apples, apples, the best you've seen.
Juice dribbling down your chin,
The thing to eat for a sparkling grin.

Apples, apples, rosy and red,
One after breakfast and one before bed.
They say that they keep the doctor away,
Healthy is the way to stay.

Apples, apples, green or red,
Good for you my mum has said.
Pop one in my pocket when I go out to play,
To keep my hunger pangs at bay.

*David Riall (10)*
*Ivy Road Primary School*


## BLUE

I like the colour blue,
I'm sure you do too.
My eyes are blue,
Some clothes are blue.
Blue is the sky
Where the clouds go by.
Blue is the colour of the sea,
It's also the colour that was made for boys,
But I don't care,
Cos it's the colour for me!

*Jennifer Eastland (11)*
*Ivy Road Primary School*

## EMILY

Emily is my treasure,
I love her lots and lots.
Of course I am very sad
When it's time for her to go.

I just lift my hand
And say goodbye,
I know I'll see her again
In a little while.

She is so sweet,
Her hand is soft.
I will always remember
The time she coughed.

Her smile is beautiful
And red,
I will remember her,
Even when she's dead.

Will it be a week?
Will it be a month
Before I see her again?
I remember when she ate her lunch.

*Eleanor Reynolds (8)*
*La Sagesse Convent Junior School*


## HIDDEN TREASURES

My hidden, valuable treasure is kept with me.
My hidden, valuable treasure is with my heart.
My hidden treasure is shiny.
My hidden, valuable treasure is never in a place where I will forget.
My hidden, valuable treasure is silver.

My hidden, valuable treasure is special to me.
My hidden, valuable treasure is that no one knows about it.
My hidden, valuable treasure is hidden somewhere.
My hidden treasure is a ring.
I will never forget my treasure.

*Megan Roberts (8)*
*La Sagesse Convent Junior School*


## HIDDEN TREASURE

'Time for bed!' shouts Mum,
'But I . . .'
'No buts! Now stop procrastinating,
Brush your teeth and into bed!
Goodnight!' she calls.

There I am, fast asleep,
Then here they come, the guys that have been in my dream.
They have been there for ever so long.
Who were they? The pirates, silly.

They had found the rusty old trunk
That had been buried under the junk.
They had found the sword, the sword of all power,
The handle is real gold and the point is made out of glass.
The ray that comes out, a girl's colour, pink!

Then they saw me, they pointed at me.
They missed.
I grabbed the treasure and ran.

With this treasure, I can live in a golden mansion,
By myself, with no mum shouting 'stop procrastinating' every night.
With this treasure I could . . .
Then I woke up.

*Briony Duff (9)*
*La Sagesse Convent Junior School*

## THE CORAL REEF

The coral reef is beautiful,
It's a treasure to me.
All the colours are wonderful,
It's a great sight to see.

How it moves,
How it sways,
It's so alive.
All the fish,
They're so great
When I see them dive.

It feels like a glass pearl,
How it swirls and twirls.
It is so fragile,
Like a princess's golden curls.

The coral reef is my treasure.

*Madeleine Otter  (8)*
*La Sagesse Convent Junior School*

## HIDDEN TREASURES

It's a mystery, it's a mystery,
How did that get there?
Once I found a pound coin
And my old teddy bear.

Next I found a dusty purse
And my missing sock,
A pen with the ink dried up
And two batteries from my alarm clock.

But best of all, my favourite book
And a necklace I thought I'd lost forever.
All these things were under my bed,
They are my hidden treasure!

*Jennie Watson  (11)*
*La Sagesse Convent Junior School*


## HIDDEN TREASURES

Pearls, rubies, others maybe,
Those are hidden treasures to me,
But there are better,
In the attic, on the floor,
Even beyond the classroom wall.
The sight of a wolf beneath the moon,
Taming a mouse
Or a squirrel,
Hugging Mum,
Running free.
When alone
At night,
Lean a little
Out of the window.
Just feel that breeze.
Explore a mansion,
Be in a ship across the sea,
Midnight feasts,
Climb a tree,
Watch a bird
Or a bee.
Those are Hidden Treasures for me!

*Clella Middleton  (8)*
*La Sagesse Convent Junior School*

## HIDDEN TREASURE

'All aboard, come on, come on, we have to get there
To find the treasure. Look, look, I can see an island.'

We have to get there quickly.
*Bump*, we have stopped.
Jump off, jump off.
Oh, it's burning.
'Get the spades,' I said,
'Get the spades,' the captain yelled.
With his patch over one eye,
The captain was digging,
Digging in different places,
Then his spade didn't go any further,
So he shouted, 'Over here, I've found it!
Over here, help me pull it out.'
He pulled and pulled and it came out.
He opened it hoping there would be lots of treasure,
But . . . nothing was there.

*Katie Crumbley (9)*
**La Sagesse Convent Junior School**


## HIDDEN TREASURES

I saw a battered old chest on the sand,
The locks were black and rusty,
It had been shaken badly in stormy seas,
So I carefully examined it.

The sand was golden and the sun was bright,
I pulled it from the sand.
The locks sprang open, I looked inside,
One bronze coin fell out. I looked at the date.

I rubbed the coin down, it sparkled in the sun,
It was out of date, but I still kept it.
I showed to Mum later on,
'It's worth a fortune!' Mum beamed.

So the battered old chest, shaken in stormy seas
And one small, scratched bronze coin,
Carefully examined by me and Mum,
Is worth a fortune!

*Francesca Ayre  (9)*
*La Sagesse Convent Junior School*


## HIDDEN TREASURE

Beneath the creaky floorboards,
Lies some hidden treasure!
Some hidden treasure I want to find!

Gold, silver, ruby rings, crowns and more surprises,
To wear and keep and act just like the Queen!

I hope there's nothing under there,
I'm sure I heard some snoring!
A dragon, a dinosaur, a ferocious alligator,
Arrrgh!

I pluck up my courage, pull up the floorboards,
I see a box, a big, gold box!
I jump down, run over, what will I find?
I open it, gold, silver . . . no!
A year's supply of *toilet roll!*

*Lucy O'Donnell  (9)*
*La Sagesse Convent Junior School*

## HIDDEN TREASURES

I opened a cute snowman-covered present,
The note said, 'Merry Christmas, Claire.'
I wondered who could have sent it,
A buzz of excitement filled the air.
I looked at it carefully,
A metal detector at Christmas from no one.

I whizzed around the garden with the metal detector,
The other presents would just have to wait,
Hold it . . . a beep . . . a beep,
I ran to get a shovel, I dug with my head buzzing.

By the time I was finished, the garden looked like a minefield,
All I found was a ring-pull, a chewing gum wrapper
And a roll of muddy foil.
Then, I started on the street!

*Claire Allen  (9)*
*La Sagesse Convent Junior School*


## HIDDEN TREASURES

Up in the attic
Behind the door,
The treasure chest lay,
Holding treasure and more.

Diamonds, rubies,
Emeralds as well,
Lay in that damp,
Dreary, cold cell.

Who could have left it?
Heaven knows who,
But whoever finds it
Will be rich, famous too.

One day it'll be found,
That rusty old box.
Everything gone,
All the magic, lost!

*Sabea Morgan  (10)*
*La Sagesse Convent Junior School*

## HIDDEN TREASURES

In the attic treasures lay,
It was an old mosaic box,
Rubies, pearls, diamonds too,
But those are not the glorious finds.

There's a map of the seven seas!
A raggy, dusty island with
Better precious stones from years ago.
Chinese silks and bamboo sticks
That lay forever cold and still.
The cobwebs hide the candle,
But no longer the light,
Yet the moon glistens in silver.

Silent, the attic will the precious secrets keep,
A childhood forever within will be.

*Hannah Abu-harb  (9)*
*La Sagesse Convent Junior School*

# HIDDEN TREASURES

Deep in the wood
Lives a green animal,
Who's dirty and fat.

He's got a secret,
An unknown secret,
A secret that's worth finding out.

He hasn't a name,
He hasn't any fame,
He's actually quite sweet.
He has a golden heart,
But no one knows,
No one knows.
Do you think that's his secret?

*Katherine Gibb  (10)*
*La Sagesse Convent Junior School*


# HIDDEN TREASURES

The stars are hidden treasures,
The moon in the sky is too,
Light is a treasure,
A sign of hope to all of the world.

Elephants are treasures too,
So are kangaroos and even spiders,
In their own unique way,
But my favourite treasures
Have to be my mum and dad!

*Genevieve Crozier  (10)*
*La Sagesse Convent Junior School*

## HIDDEN TREASURE

The man with the beard,
The eye patch and cap,
Stared long and hard
At the cross on the map.

He hummed and he ha'd
At the way to walk,
If only the picture of
The parrot could talk.

He packed his bag,
His spade and pick
And set off walking
At a merry lick.

He walked for weeks,
Months and years,
Until his boots
Were full of leaks.

Then one day he saw and heard
A large cawing jackdaw bird.
He chased the bird which had flown,
Until he saw a cross marked with bones.

He dug and dug for a day and night
And stepped back full of fright,
For there was a box with big, rusty locks
And skull and bones stared back and mocked.

He opened the chest and stood back in glee,
He had found the treasures of the legend, McGee.

*Jessica Major  (8)*
*La Sagesse Convent Junior School*

## HIDDEN TREASURE

Going under water,
Looking for treasure trove,
'Tut, tut,' I hear,
Then there's a . . .
Shadow, big, black and mean.
I sit and wonder, 'What have I seen?'
I swim and swim until I can swim no more,
I looked down, fourteen letters in my head -
H, I, D, D, E, N, T, R, E, A, S, U, R, E.

H   iding in the sand,
I   n the Atlantic Ocean,
D   own, down deep,
D   epth completely out,
E   verything so spectacular,
N   o one ever knew . . .

'Chomp, chomp,' I hear.
I turn around and see there's a
Big, fat shark heading for me.
Strangely, the shark flies overhead,
So I finish off the letters instead.

T   ime to open the chest,
R   ound and round I float,
E   veryone knows that it's not always good.
A   h - rich, money,
S   o let's not get our hopes up,
U   nexpectedly I open it,
R   iches, riches,
E   verything's mine.

*Naomi Hicks  (8)*
*La Sagesse Convent Junior School*

## HIDDEN TREASURES

Hooray, hooray!
We're going to the beach today.
Bring our shovel and the rake,
Hum, what else shall we take?

Here we are running,
Running over the sand.
Wait a minute, what is this?
It's a map, a treasure one.

A pirate's map, look, a ship,
Should we follow this?
It looks like a good trip.

With our shovel and our rake,
Quick run, or we'll be late.
On the ship, over the beam,
Ah, a pirates' boat, what a loud scream.

'Ha, ha, ha,' said Captain Pegleg,
'We will get the treasure.
Give us the map.'
Never, never.

Dig, dig, we're on the sand,
We've found it. Open it, open it.
And in it was gold and silver,
Rubies and rings.
Hip, hip, hooray. We gave it back
To the rightful owner.
Oh, what a wonderful day.

*Beth Watson  (10)*
*La Sagesse Convent Junior School*

## HIDDEN TREASURE

I was looking for treasure,
Searching in the garden,
Looking for something special,
Turning over leaves.

I found a brown, shiny shell,
It was round like a nut.
I held it in my hand, turning it over,
Holding it up to the sun.

When I looked closer,
Bubbles came out of one end.
It made my hand all slimy,
I wondered why a shell was blowing bubbles at me?

I held my hand very still,
Looking at it for a long time.
Two feelers came out slowly,
They were like grey, slimy twigs, with eyes on the end.

I watched a little longer,
Two more twigs with eyes popped out.
I looked at them closely.
They looked back at me.

I had been looking for treasure,
But the treasure I found was hidden,
A secret creature
Hiding inside his home.

*Daisy Abraham  (8)*
*La Sagesse Convent Junior School*

## HIDDEN TREASURES

Stranded on a shipwreck,
Far away from home,
Surrounded by the silver,
Moonlit waves of the sea,
Nowhere to flee to,
Except an island about a mile away.

Suddenly, white, sparkling footprints
Appeared, bobbing on the waves.
I jumped into the water and swam
After the glistening footprints.
The footprints led me to the island,
They carried on over a hot, sandy hill,
Into a jungle.

The sun was rising like a
Yellow beach ball in the sky.
I ran after the footprints,
For they were fading fast into
The shadows of the palm trees.

Where the footprints stopped,
Like they needed more energy.
I found a coconut, it was yellow and brown,
A glint of sun reflected off it.
I pulled it out of the ground.
To my amazement, it wasn't
A yellow and brown coconut.
It was a battered, old treasure chest.

*Megan Dale (9)*
*La Sagesse Convent Junior School*

## HIDDEN TREASURES

Hidden treasures may be precious,
Maybe they are under the ocean,
Maybe high on the land unnoticed,
We should really care for them all.

Could be gold buried in the sand,
Or just a rose that no one looks at.
Even the air which no one thinks about,
Only if they were studying it.

But most of all we have to think,
Nature is the important one!
Without somewhere to stand on, like the Earth,
We may be falling, or not even alive.
Everyone must stop destroying the world,
And please never forget love,
And I hope everyone listens to that!

*Rebecca Hsu Webb-Mitchell  (9)*
*La Sagesse Convent Junior School*


## HIDDEN TREASURES

Hidden treasure underground,
Hidden treasure, can't be found.
A crinkled map all tattered and torn,
I cannot read it, it's all worn.
So where's the treasure?
Where can it be,
Over land or over sea?

*Jessica McClean  (10)*
*La Sagesse Convent Junior School*

## HIDDEN TREASURES

Buried deep, deep under the ground,
Treasure had been hidden for years
And had not been found.
In that black, dreary treasure chest,
Big and round.

I dug, dug deep into the ground
To search for that treasure
That had not yet been found.
I stretched my arm as far as it would reach,
I fell through and let out a fearful screech.

'Where was I?' was the first thing I thought,
I did not get the treasure,
I was thinking of the things I could have bought.

*Abbie Bowman (10)*
*La Sagesse Convent Junior School*


## HIDDEN TREASURES

Digging in the sand,
I feel something under my hand.
What can it be? I'll have to dig and see.
A huge, battered box with rusty, iron locks.
What can it be? I'll have to open it and see.
Creaking, cracking, open wide,
One thousand sparkling jewels inside,
Sparkling, glittering in the light,
I can hardly believe this lovely sight.
Princess's treasures from afar,
I'll keep them safely in my car.

*Natalie-Emma Weatherley (9)*
*La Sagesse Convent Junior School*

## NOBLE JOHN'S TREASURE HUNT

Noble John is noble,
Noble John is strong,
Noble John goes round the place
At his digging pace
With a smile upon his noble face.
His thing is to be a treasure hunter
And because he's the pride of Merseyside
And wants a good reputation,
For Noble John is modest,
Noble John is strong,
Treasures quake and start to shake
When Noble comes along.

*Jessica Hall  (11)*
*La Sagesse Convent Junior School*


## HIDDEN TREASURES

Hidden treasures under the sand,
Or maybe on land or on sea,
But most people think treasure is
All gold and silver, but it's not.
Some treasure is your loved ones.

Because you don't always have your loved ones,
But you'll mostly always have money,
Make the most of your family and loved ones,
Because they may not always be there for you.

*Charlotte Bennetts  (10)*
*La Sagesse Convent Junior School*

# HIDDEN TREASURE

Down, down under the sea in a submarine,
I could be rich, but then I could be poor.

I wish, I wish I could find this treasure.
I'll say my magic word and then it will
Suddenly appear in a puff of smoke.

As I was sleeping on the seabed,
I heard a noise, a booming noise and
When I woke I saw a light,
I ran over to the treasure and
Tried to work out the code for the treasure chest.
Was it 2-4-6? No, it was 6-4-8.
I opened the chest to find rings, necklaces and earrings
Made of pure gold, encrusted with
Emeralds, diamonds, rubies and sapphires.

With excitement, I steered my submarine
Up and up to the surface and showed everyone,
And this was a legend and I mean, a legend.

*Lucy Jobson  (11)*
*La Sagesse Convent Junior School*


# THE TREASURE IN MY LIFE

My treasure is something that I keep in my heart,
My treasure is the most special thing in my life,
It is so special that it is guarded
By the soldiers that live in my heart.
It is more special than jewels or pearls,
My treasure is a special memory.

*Chloe Grace Cullen  (8)*
*La Sagesse Convent Junior School*

## HIDDEN TREASURES!

You don't have to look far
To find a shooting star.
You don't root about
To watch the sun come out.
You don't need special powers
To see beauty in flowers.
You don't need lots of money
To watch bees gather honey.
You don't need to say please,
To watch the leaves change colour
                        on the trees.
You don't need to pay for pleasure,
Just look around and you'll find
The treasure!

*Martha Craven  (9)*
*La Sagesse Convent Junior School*


## HIDDEN TREASURES

Hidden treasures are many things,
Not just gold or diamond rings.
For my dog Eddie, it is a bone,
For my sister, her mobile phone,
To my mother it means new clothes,
For my grandma, her garden hose,
To my granddad, it's what he cooks,
For my dad, it's all his books.
Now for me, let me see,
Of course, it must be my family.

*Emma Blackshaw  (8)*
*La Sagesse Convent Junior School*

## HIDDEN TREASURES

Shipwrecked on a deserted island,
Alone by a tall palm tree
With just my pack strapped to my back,
I pick up a box thrown from the ship,
Inside was a map of the island
I was on.
It showed a box of treasure
Under the ground where I stood.
So I dug a hole,
Just like a mole.
I opened the chest,
Inside was gold,
Silver and jewels.

*Sophia Spiropoulos (8)*
*La Sagesse Convent Junior School*


## HIDDEN TREASURES

There's some hidden treasure,
Special and unique to me.
Not pirates' gold buried deep,
But very near to me.
A wonderful kind of treasure,
Not worth any money at all,
A treasure you just can't buy,
But kind and gentle, loving too.
So guess who?
This treasure is my mum,
That's who!

*Rachael Gourley (8)*
*La Sagesse Convent Junior School*

# HIDDEN TREASURES

I found a map of hidden treasures,
I found a map waiting for me,
I found a map right over the sea.

I jumped, I leaped to find it,
I crawled, I prowled to find it,
I walked, I ran to find it.

I went over roads to find it,
I jumped over toads to find it,
I ducked under loads to find it.

I went over there,
I went to stare,
But I guess that treasure was . . .
*Me!*

*Katie Gilfillan  (9)*
*La Sagesse Convent Junior School*


# MY SPECIAL FRIEND

My special friend has big, green eyes,
My special friend has tiny little feet.

My special friend has sharp teeth,
My special friend has a fur coat.

My special friend wakes me up in the night,
My special friend breaks my ornaments,

But I still love her, no matter what.
My special friend is a cat.

*Emma Donohoe  (7)*
*La Sagesse Convent Junior School*

# HIDDEN TREASURES

We explored the shore,
The rocks and the pools,
Nobody there to spoil our day,
Only the sounds of the birds and sea,
We played our games from breakfast till tea.

We may have been the first humans for hundreds of years
To find the caves well hidden.
We had to be brave to climb inside.
I think we were, don't you?

The silence was eerie, it was hard to see,
Something was shining in front of me.
We stretched out our hands and to our surprise,
We had found the most beautiful treasure,
My friend and me.

*Amy Smith  (9)*
*La Sagesse Convent Junior School*


# THE TREASURES OF SPRING

My hidden treasure's spring.
Flowers, bulbs, daffodils,
grow out of the ground.
Baby animals come out of
their mother's wombs,
Birds start to make nests,
Leaves start to grow on trees,
Baby lambs play,
Bulbs push their way up through the soil.
My treasure is spring.

*Lisa Chambers  (8)*
*La Sagesse Convent Junior School*

## MEMORIES

Doing jigsaws with Grandma Johnstone, matching all the pieces,
Playing with Winston all day long and giving him lots of kisses!
Going to Turkey, having lots of fun,
Playing in the sand and sea, underneath the sun.

I've been to Edinburgh Zoo, lots to see and do,
The animals are lovely,
But my favourite has to be,
A monkey, because it acts like me!

Blackpool lights were a sight to see,
A donkey ride was special to me!

My hidden treasures are memories.

*Amelia Armstrong  (8)*
*La Sagesse Convent Junior School*


## HIDDEN TREASURE

We set off to find the treasure,
The ancient map said east.
We looked for the coconut island.
There it was, gleaming in the sun.
I smiled with excitement and the boat whizzed closer.
Closer and closer we came to the coconut island,
Burning sand pressed on our boats.
One by one, we touched the chest,
We clenched it in our hands.
We hid it in our ship
And as we floated on the sea, I said,
Our mission has been completed.

*Eram Ahmad  (10)*
*La Sagesse Convent Junior School*

## MY TREASURE

My treasure is red,
My treasure is guarded by a hundred men,
My treasure is lovely,
My treasure is sparkling.
Do you know what it is?
It's a ruby!

*Charlotte Hudson  (7)*
*La Sagesse Convent Junior School*

## ELSIE

Our dog Elsie is a puppy that is good and sometimes bad
She eats the furniture and your toys
She likes to have a go at other dogs
She lies on her back asking to have her belly rubbed
She likes to bark at he dogs next door.

She is a small rat-like dog that can fit through our cat flap
She has a stubby, little tail that is often wagging
Her hind legs don't bend so she bounces through the grass
Her ears don't stick up but flop over
She has sharp teeth and claws.

She is bad because she likes to eat her bed
Her toys have to be strong or she eats them quickly
She likes to run to the nearest stranger and jump up on them
She is good because she is obedient
She will sleep all night
She will always come and greet you with a loving smile.

We all love Elsie
Well I do!

*Rachel Lewis  (10)*
*Newcastle Preparatory School*

# TOAD TAIL

There was a young lad named Bernard who
Whilst walking down the road
Went into a magic shop
And got swallowed by a toad
The toad was large and greedy
Bernard satisfied his need
With hunger pangs now disappeared
He felt very well indeed!
Not so Bernard . . .
Inside the toad now dark and dreary
His future looking somewhat bleak
His prospects far from cheery
But then an idea sprang to mind
If I tickle Toady's tummy
He may decide the joke's on him
Spit me out where it's warm and sunny
Alas the plan backfired
Toady reached out for his wand
Cast a spell on our poor Bernard
Now at the bottom of the pond.

*Edward McDonald  (11)*
*Newcastle Preparatory School*


# MY MUSIC

The albums on the shelf in my room
are what my mum says are dirt and gloom.
From Lincoln Park to the Offspring lot,
Mum's music's just rubbish and glot.
Oh the music that we've got at home
just makes you wonder, will it ever go?
I hate the likes of Hear'Say and Steps

the bands I could go to and swim to the depths.
The Beatles, Blur, Wheatus and Oasis
'Tosh,' my dad says, as he thumbs his braces.
The singles in my mum's day were 50p
she says that's the way it bloomin' well should be.
She looks at the band on the CD case
'My, you've got such bad taste.'

*Edward Smith  (11)*
*Newcastle Preparatory School*


## THE ORDEAL

I stagger back, thoughts rushing through my head,
Will I ever see my family again?
Everything suddenly turns into a fantasy,
I feel like I'm in a game,
Waiting till the screen says 'Game over,'
I am thrown back into reality as another fiend falls down,
Bullets fly past me as the enemy launches another brutal attack,
I can see the trench and I'm very relieved when I find myself
covered in mud and unable to see the enemy.
A few hours later the war finally ends and another close victory,
The remaining few climb out of their holes to make sure,
We go back to the quarters to get the carts,
After some much needed rest we return to the field,
Stinking bodies cover the grass as we begin to clear up,
More letters given to their loved ones,
More graves, more deaths, more pain,
More companions lost,
I wonder if this ordeal will ever end,
Probably never . . .

*Jaspreet Sanghera  (10)*
*Newcastle Preparatory School*

# FOOTBALL

Football is a world sport,
There are teams from London to Singapore,
They all have one thing in common they love to kick a ball.
The ball is round, not square or oval,
White not black or green,
And when you're at a football match you cheer for your team.
Football is a great sport,
I wish it could be me,
Playing in the matches and getting a huge pay fee!
Matches last for 90 minutes 45 each way,
And fans of the Premier League love the style of play.
There are eleven players in a team,
To be one of them would be my dream,
To show my team had done really well,
I'd have a cup and winner's medal.
To play in the Premier League would be a fairy tale,
But not if I was suddenly put up for sale!
Every player's dream is to win a world cup,
That is the greatest test,
It shows to everyone your team is the best.

*James Smith  (11)*
*Newcastle Preparatory School*


# MY HOLIDAY POEM

I like to go on holiday
Where the sun shines all day long
I try to leave my family but they always tag along
I'd like to go more often but I have to go to school
I'd rather be on holiday, swimming in the pool
When we go on holiday we leave our work behind

And concentrate on having fun and being wined and dined.
Now I am on holiday there's so many things to do
Excuse me now I have to go to be beside the sea
I'll play down there till half-past three and then I'll have my tea
But all too soon it's time to leave, we have to go back home
But wait, I think I have time to write another poem.

*Kimberley Hay  (10)*
*Newcastle Preparatory School*


## SICK SID

I had a sick horse, I took him to the vet,
I said 'Would you treat him he is my only pet.'
'I'll do what I can, but that won't be much,
you really shouldn't keep a horse in a rabbit hutch!'

I raced to the shop to buy him some food
trotted back to the vet and said 'Look at my pet.'
'I've told you once and I'll tell you again,
you shouldn't keep a horse in a baby pen.'

I cantered to the farm to get some hay
galloped back to the vet to see what he'd say.
'He's not a rabbit, he's not a kid,
he's a horse of course and his name is Sid!'

So he got a jab and Sid was sad
he cried and said his head was like lead
and wanted to go to bed with his ted.
'He's ill,' I said, 'please give him a pill.'
The vet shook his head and gave him a tonic.
I gave him the drink and Sid with a wink
is no longer sick - *he's supersonic!*

*Bradley Murphy  (9)*
*Newcastle Preparatory School*

## MY SCHOOL

My school is a haunted house to me
The teachers never leave me be.
Where boys fight and girls write
On the ceiling where spiders crawl.
Where graffiti stains our clean walls
When we pick teams in the playground.
Whatever the game might be
There's always someone who's last.
And it's usually me.
Mondays are usually boring
My friend's away, and it's pouring
I'm late for school again.
I overslept, so I blamed it on the bus.
So why is everyone making a fuss?
Sausages, carrots
Cooked to a treat
Ham, stew and haggis
Or simple minced meat.
Oh I wish I could go home to eat
That's pretty much it
But I bet the teachers enjoy every bit.

*Lucy Wright (10)*
*Newcastle Preparatory School*


## FOOTBALL CRAZY, FOOTBALL MAD

'Football is for wimps,' I heard a big kid say
'I'll show you who's a wimp if you care to stay and play.'
To my surprise before my eyes the big kid said, 'OK.
My name is Dan and I'm not a fan, but I'll give this game a go.'
The deal was sealed, we hit the field and heard the whistle blow.
He wasn't bad, this big, tall lad, but I thought he was my foe.
But he gave a call and passed the ball and I put it in the net.

He passed lots more for me to score, till I was four goals in his debt.
We won the game, I'm glad he came
Cos he puts two goals in that same net.
Now that kid Dan is football's biggest fan
That is plain to see
That big lad is not at all bad
He's as footy mad as me!

*Josh Walton  (10)*
*Newcastle Preparatory School*


## PORTIA

She is very small
When she is curled up in a ball
She gets so deep in my covers
When she is asleep
She always wants to eat
Her jelly and meat
She's constantly running around my feet.

She mostly likes to play every day
She scratches at my door
When she wants to play some more
Her eyes are nice and green
But they are not mean
And at night they always shine bright
Just like the moonlight.

She uses her feet
To jump onto her seat
That is where she sits
When she looks out onto the street
Meow, meow, and meow, now she wants to play
My pet cat Portia will have to wait another day.

*Oliver Stedman  (10)*
*Newcastle Preparatory School*

# MY HOUSE IS A ZOO

'Mum, Mum!
There's a dog in the lounge
There's a monkey in the fridge
There's a rat in the floorboards
There's an alien up the chimney
There's a chimpanzee under my bed
There's a gorilla in the shed
There's a lion playing my PlayStation
There's an alligator down the toilet
There's fish and swans in the bath
There's a crocodile in the shower
There's a cow in the yard
There's a mouse in my bedside cabinet
There's a horse in your bed
There's a cheetah playing cards
There's a pig in the sink
There's hens on the roofs
There's a cat in my room
And he ate all my fish
There's a caterpillar on the computer
There's a butterfly under the sofa
There's a dog eating popcorn
I can't stand it any more.'

*Christopher Jaffray (10)*
*Newcastle Preparatory School*


# MY BIRTHDAY

Today is my birthday, I'm so happy and glad
My mum has gone completely mad
They wake me up at 6 o'clock
To give me presents and an alarm clock.

We all have fun on this special day
Travelling into town to see a play
We laugh and joke until we hear someone say
'Do you realise, we've got the wrong day?'
My birthday is tomorrow.

*Lucy Tweedlie  (9)*
*Newcastle Preparatory School*

## FIRE

The sparkling, singing, crackles of flames,
The gleaming light of God.
The heart warms you like the sun,
You have to tear away your eyes from -
The beautiful colours of blue, gold and green.

The birth of fire is like a baby stream that flows -
Across to the roaring sea.
The death of fire is like water drying up.
But mid fire, with plenty of food -
Is like a child, skipping and jumping in the sun.

The burning of wood and the smell of smoke is the darkness of fire,
That will lead you to your death,
You just try and see, but the flickering flames in the ark
Will guide you and set you free.
The fire speaks - feed me, watch me, get warm -
But leave me alone!

*William Ralph  (10)*
*Newcastle Preparatory School*

## MY BROTHER

My brother's a brat
He's also rather fat
He can't fit through the garden gate
Because he's rather overweight.
He's as big as a barge
He's quite over large
He's as thick as a post
And is scared of a ghost.
He swims like a log
Did I mention he's as fat as a hog?
He's as slow as a worm
He goes to school at half term.
He looks like a tortoise with a stomach ache
He would run as soon as look at a snake
He's rather slow as we've already said
But there's something else
Oh yeah, his big, fat head
That just about sums up my brother
He's a big, fat lump of blubber.

*David Breakey (10)*
*Newcastle Preparatory School*

## SCHOOL

Waking up at seven, going out at eight
Feeling lousy as I go through the gate
Walking in the classroom, acting like a fool
Why, oh why do we have to go to school?
Why, oh why do we have to go to school?
Now the day has started, lessons have begun
Sitting down to maths, it really isn't fun.

Working like a sloth, looking like one too
Why, oh why do we have to go to school?
Coming up to lunchtime, I kind of like school dinner
Since last night I think I've got thinner
Now we have English, the day is such a drag
A little kid is pestering me, he really is a nag.
And now it's time to go back home and I think all in all
That after some consideration, school's not too bad at all.

*Joshua Hughes (9)*
*Newcastle Preparatory School*

## NO POEMS

I've been set a task, it's a total shocker,
My teacher wants a poem,
I want to play virtual soccer,
Sat in my room at home.

I've eaten my tea, it must be done
I sit at my desk and think,
I've had a play, I've had some fun
I know I will get a drink.

The page is white
My pencil is still
I've got to write somethin'
Or I'll be here all night
A knock on the door, it might be Bill
Never mind the poem, the book's in the bin.

*Mark Hall (9)*
*Newcastle Preparatory School*

## SCIENCE

Science is good,
Science is cool,
Science is fun,
With science you rule.

Surfing the web will help us learn,
To find that not all gold glistens
All you need to find out facts
Is to watch, ask and listen.

With Bunsen burners
We heat things up,
And pour the mixture
From the measuring cup.

In the science lab take care
To make sure you don't get burnt,
Listen to what the teacher says
And remember all you've learned.

Experiments galore,
Oh, won't we have fun,
Explode a stink bomb
Then let's all run.

Einstein, Pasteur and Madame Curie
Teach science in our class.
With the aid of TV and video
Our exams we all should pass.

*Patrick Smith  (11)*
*Newcastle Preparatory School*

## MY COMPUTER

My computer hypnotises me
I'm in a deep trace: struck dumb with fear
While using its binding games and maze like Internet
Every click of a key sends me willingly
In a new direction, hitting more dead ends
It talks to me, stalking me
It's like a venomous spider, that tangles me in its
World wide web; a world as gigantic as the universe
I lose track of time and place
Like a tarantula it catches me
I'm one of its many fearful preys
I still take the risk of dying in its deadly games,
Because it's thrilling and adventurous
As I surf the web
I am hunting for facts,
Exploring the web like a bounty hunter
Searching a vast, empire-like jungle
Hoping to be the victor but not the victim.

*Tony Wong  (11)*
*Newcastle Preparatory School*


## A CHILD PRAYER

I say my prayers and hop into bed
Straighten the pillow and smooth and spread
And leave the room with Jesus beside me in bed.
Him and His angels will sing me to sleep
Like a good shepherd leading his sheep
And we slip off to the Land of Nod
Just wee little and the Son of God.

*John Weekes  (10)*
*Newcastle Preparatory School*

## SEASONS

A weak and watery sun low in the winter sky,
Not a green shoot to be seen upon branches high,
Crows cawing, icy winds whistling, frost deep in the ground,
Brown and soggy last year's leaves lying all around.

Snowdrops pushing upwards, lambs bleating, first signs of spring
High up in the branches the birds start to sing,
Daffodils blowing in the breeze, pale green shoots unfurling
The sun grows warmer, bees buzzing, swallows wheeling, whirling.

Full sun high in the sky, the smell of new mown hay,
Picnics, tennis, swimming each long and lazy, summer day,
Trees in full leaf, corn turning golden, combines everywhere
Beaches crowded, soft, white sand, babies running bare.

First autumn frosts, blackberries ripening, harvest gathered in
Leaves turning red and brown, conkers falling fat and thin
Hunting horns sound on distant hills,
Cattle brought in from far off fields
The end of the year is near.

*Andrew Robson  (10)*
*Newcastle Preparatory School*


## MY ANIMALS

My rabbit, Dillon is fluffy and small
He lives in a run next to my garden wall
My dog is called Glen, he's shiny and black
If I throw him a stick, he always brings it back.
With ponies and horses and cats two or three
My dad says our house is a menagerie.

*Alexander Gray  (9)*
*Newcastle Preparatory School*

## MY TEACHERS

My maths teacher can't count
My French teacher can't speak French
My English teacher doesn't know the vowels
My geography teacher doesn't know where London is
My history teacher thinks the year is 1805
My music teacher doesn't know what a violin is
My science teacher hasn't a clue what planet we're on
My RE teacher thinks Jews don't exist
My art teacher has permanent paint everywhere
My Latin teacher doesn't know what Latin is
My technology teacher thinks cardboard is dangerous
My PE teacher has never heard of sport
My swimming teacher is scared of the water
My VR teacher can't even do VR
The worst is my games teacher - because he picks his nose!

*Laura Forrest  (10)*
*Newcastle Preparatory School*


## IN MY GRANDMA'S WARDROBE

In my grandma's wardrobe are many secrets.
In my grandma's wardrobe are the echoes of long-forgotten thoughts.
In my grandma's wardrobe are things from when they wed.
they were happy times that would soon be filled with dread,
when the war came.
In my grandma's wardrobe are slippers with bunny ears,
old handbags and diaries filled with a thousand memories.
In my grandma's wardrobe are the skins of sheep.
In my grandma's wardrobe are things to make you weep.
In my grandma's wardrobe are the ashes of my grandpa, in a shoe box.

*Benet Plowden  (10)*
*Newcastle Preparatory School*

## MUM, MUM, THERE'S A ZOO IN MY ROOM

Mum, Mum, there's a monster in my bed
It has huge eyes and it's eating my cat's head.
Mum, Mum, there's a lion in my room
And it's eating my books.
Mum, Mum, there a giraffe in my room
But guess what, it smashed a hole in my roof!
Mum, Mum, there's an ape in my room
And it's sitting on my telly.
Mum, Mum, there's a polar bear in my room
And it's sooooooo cold.
Mum, Mum, I think I've got the whole zoo in my room,
But the most destructive of all is my sister.
*Heeellllppppp!*

*Aria Rabet  (10)*
*Newcastle Preparatory School*


## I MET A DRAGON

I met a dragon by the sea
He tried to run away from me
But then I shouted, 'Stop
I won't say a word
Not even to a bird
If you tell me your secret
I need to know why
You dragons can fly.'
He turned his head and looked at me
And said, 'Young man this I can tell
We dragons can breathe fire as well.'

*Ben Howe  (9)*
*Newcastle Preparatory School*

## THE TRAMP

There he sits like a dark shadow just like the look on his face
You also would be very surprised if he was part of the human race.
There he lies on the path sneering at the passers-by then he
                                                    starts to wonder
If his life is a stupid lie
But then one young boy passed, he didn't sneer at all
No, he didn't sneer at all at the young passer-by
Who reminded him of something else
Maybe the family that he once had
And the search for them was driving him very and awfully mad.

*David Kebell (10)*
*Newcastle Preparatory School*


## REMOTE CONTROL CARS

What do they do? They jump to the top
What do they do? They fall off the drop
What do they do? They brake all the time
What do they do? They smash and make crimes
What do they do? They spin all day
What do they do? They turn all ways
What do they do? They stop at the lights
What do they do? They bash and have fights
What do they do? They burn along the road
What do they do? They put it on turbo mode
What do they do? They skid round the bend
What do they do? They always extend
What do they do? They spring up high
What do I do? I say goodbye.

*Declan McDonough (9)*
*St Alban's RC Primary School*

## MACBETH

School is boring, school's not neat
Make it melt beneath our feet.

Add a head teacher's hair
To make him go spare.
Add a slop of custard
Plus a dollop of mustard.

School is boring, school's not neat
Make it melt beneath our feet.

Add a broken hardback chair
Add it to St Alban's fair.
Add a mouldy apple tree
With a grey, mushy pea.

School is boring, school's not neat
Make it melt beneath our feet.

Add an old door handle
Add a school baptismal candle.
Add a printer and a scanner
And an old school banner.

School is boring, school's not neat
Make it melt beneath our feet.

*Michael Taylor  (10)*
*St Alban's RC Primary School*


## WORM

Under miles of mud a slimy worm hid
It jumped to the top with a bottle of pop
I picked it up with a shovel
And mixed it up in a muddle

I missed my dinner and I got thinner
I looked at the worm and it started to squirm
I ate the worm and it lasted the whole term
I will never forget the time I swallowed that bundle of slime.

*Sophie Naylor (10)*
*St Alban's RC Primary School*


## MACBETH

School is boring, school is hard work
Let us all burn our skirts.

In we throw our teacher's hair,
And caretakers, grizzly bears,
Time-consuming homework books,
All the teachers with bad looks.

School is boring, school is hard work
Let us all burn our skirts.

There goes all the lumpy custard,
Add to it the spicy mustard,
There goes runny paint,
And Mrs Rogers' strong mints.

School is boring, school is hard work
Let us all burn our skirts.

Long legs of teacher,
Head of stupid preacher,
Ancient, mouldy toilet seat,
Teacher's book all complete.

School is boring, school is hard work
Let us all burn our skirts.

*Catherine Pidgeon (11)*
*St Alban's RC Primary School*

## MACBETH

Go school, go with our teachers
Make them look like ugly creatures

Text books, pens into the cauldron
Chips of stone never lay hands on
In the hall, on the stage
7 out of 20, I'm in rage.

Go school, with our teachers
Make them look like ugly creatures

In they go Oxford dictionary
Rather have a good game of Pictionary
Round the cauldron all they go
Lots of bones from teachers' toes.

Go school, go with our teachers
Make them look like ugly creatures

In the staff room drinking tea
Non shatter ruler it was free
Still in goes Key Stage 2
Please Miss can I go to the loo?

Go school, go with our teachers
Make them look like ugly creatures.

*Laura Graham  (10)*
*St Alban's RC Primary School*


## THE WINTER WIND

The winter wind blows chilly and cold
The summer now is growing old,
White, cold frost lies sparkling on the ground,
The dark nights creep sneakily in without a sound.

People huddle around their firesides burning bright
Lights twinkle through the cold crisp night
The Christmas season is on its way
Look out! Here comes Santa on his sleigh.

*Ashley Hall  (10)*
*St Alban's RC Primary School*


## JUNGLE

As the track starts to fade away,
As night swallows day,
Scrambling over the forest floor,
Out of a leaf, a fragment is torn,
Then I see the army ants,
Ripping, tearing, at other plants.
When we walk into a clearing,
Poor Jim is sent careering,
Then it hits me and I see,
A leopard standing over me!
And just when it's about to bite,
Snarling in its own delight,
It falls off me, and it cries,
I think it's just been tranquillised.
And as I climb up to my feet,
And as I say 'Wow, that was neat.'
I look back down to the ground,
And see it sleeping without a sound,
I turn and congratulate my mate,
For I nearly befall my fate,
Soon we come back to the air strip,
And that was the end of my jungle trip.

*Richard Humphries  (9)*
*St Alban's RC Primary School*

## OUT OF MY WINDOW

Out of my window,
The wind's going mad,
Just like an old man who's very sad,
The children are happy,
Sometimes they're wearing a nappy,
The dogs are running all over the place,
I must tie my shoelace,
Look, there's a ball,
It's David's who's very tall,
Out of my window, there's no worry,
It's just like eating a red-hot curry.

*Sarah Woodward (9)*
*St Alban's RC Primary School*


## LEAVES

Leaves swish and dance
Burning colours
Leaves twirl, spiral,
Softly under your feet
Leaves tumble, spin and blow.

*Andrew Buglass (7)*
*St Alban's RC Primary School*


## THE ICE SKATER

The ice skater is as graceful as a dove,
She glides along the slippery ice like a smooth iron.
She moves as softly and as quietly as a mouse,
She twirls and swirls like a spinning top.

She dances and prances like a baby deer,
She is as elegant as a swan.
She happily humps in the wind like she's trying to fly,
When she's jumping, she always smiles a smile as big as she can.

*Katie Crosby  (9)*
*St Alban's RC Primary School*


## BIRDS

What are birds? They're big and small
What are birds? They're black and white
What are birds? Things that sing
What are birds? They have nests

What are birds? Crows and magpies
What do birds do? Fly and eat worms?
Birds are fun, I would like to have one.

*Richard Hoggins  (10)*
*St Alban's RC Primary School*


## MY PET

My pet is brown
He is really large
My pet is dead funny
Tickles me by licking my feet
He drops the ball on my lap
Can you guess what my pet is?
My pet is a dog!

*Aimee Varey  (9)*
*St Alban's RC Primary School*

## WINNIE THE POOH

Pooh Bear is fat and he likes honey
Then there's Yellow Rabbit, a rather moody bunny
Owl is very wise
Tigger can bounce up to the skies.
Piglet hardly makes a sound
Roo also likes to bounce around
Kanga could tidy the nursery all day
Eeyore's tail is forever coming away
Beaver isn't mentioned much
All have a loving touch.

*Maxine Davies  (10)*
*St Alban's RC Primary School*


## THE SEA

The sea is blue
Fish are grey and white
Boats are brown
That float on the sea
Waves and shells come into the shore
People swim, seagulls fly over the waves.

*David Carter  (8)*
*St Alban's RC Primary School*


## FOOTBALL

Football is fun for all
Always running with the ball
Get a red card
You are barred
Score a goal

Trip and fall
Take a free kick
Here comes Mick
When the game is over
Everyone is sober.

*Lee Oxborough (10)*
*St Alban's RC Primary School*

## THE STARRY NIGHT

As the moon and stars at night
Waiting until it gets bright.
The man looks up at the sky
Watching the stars float by
The stars twinkle like diamonds
High in the sky.

*David Rogers (9)*
*St Alban's RC Primary School*

## AT DAWN

At dawn there are colours in the sky
Yellow, red, orange and maybe purple.
The trees and grass are black shadows
A flicker of light
Comes from the east
In a few minutes
The shadows start to disappear.

*Lee Robson (9)*
*St Alban's RC Primary School*

## MY FAMILY

My mum is quite fat,
She once sat upon my cat,
It squealed and screamed and ran away,
And came back another day.

My mum once made a cup of tea,
Look there is a bee,
It goes buzz and it's so bright,
My mum goes zzzzzzz all through the night.

My dad likes going boo, hiss, boo,
And every time he does it he gets the flu,
He stays in bed and never gets fed,
And there's my sister laughing off her head.

*Leanne Roche  (9)*
*St Alban's RC Primary School*

## THE ICE SKATER

She is as graceful as a swan
As elegant as a dove
She is as quiet as a mouse
As beautiful as a rose
She skates as though walking on a hot day
Not on ice, but on a path.
See her fly across the ice like a bird
See her sway back and forwards
Like daffodils in the breeze.

*Kathryn Close  (8)*
*St Alban's RC Primary School*

## I HAVE A FRIEND

I have a friend called Sue Lee
Who is as fair as can be!
She's got curly hair
Like a bear
She's got deep, dark eyes
Like some pies
She's got a small, round nose
Like a rose
She's got a nice, smooth chin
Like a blunt pin
And cute, little ears
Like pointy spears.

*Avril Cathcart  (8)*
*St Alban's RC Primary School*


## OUT OF MY WINDOW

Out of my window I can see,
The neighbour's dog Lucky looking at me,
St Oswald's Church and its priest, Ken,
Blaine and David's gang which number ten.
Claire's house down the street,
Then my dad taking Joe for a treat.
As they come back Dad says, 'What a save!'
As a football passes my fish's grave.
Then the day ends all is said,
It's now time for me to go to bed.

*Georgia Lennie  (8)*
*St Alban's RC Primary School*

# THE FOOTBALLER

He moves
As swiftly as the wind
He's got studs on the bottom of his boots
That are as sharp as nails.
The front of his boots are like a witch's hat
He can kick the ball as high as the clouds
And he is as strong as an ox
The football pitch is very muddy
He sometimes slides
He gets the ball
Shoots in the net
The crowd roar *'Goal!'*

*Aaron Melton  (8)*
*St Alban's RC Primary School*

# HIDDEN TREASURES

Hidden treasures lots to find, there's all sorts of different kinds
In the garden hide and seek, is it worth a little peak?
Chocolates, sweets and candy, yum
Molly, Emma, Andy eating gum.
I give up I can't see a thing
I bet your mum's hidden them in the biscuit tin.
See I told you I was right
Hurry! Hurry! Switch on the light.
Look at the treasures we have found
Won't we have fun passing them round?

*Jennifer Johnson  (9)*
*St Alban's RC Primary School*

## MACBETH

Double, double, smells of trouble,
Make the teachers into bubble.
All our uniform not worn,
Ripped and smelly, arms are torn.
Double, double, smells of trouble,
Make the teachers into bubble.
Time-consuming homework book,
Goodbye teachers, goodbye cooks.
Double, double, smells of trouble,
Make the teachers into bubble.
Trash my pencil, ruler too,
Add headmaster's smelly shoe.
Double, double, smells of trouble,
Make the teachers into bubble.
Scrap the tests and register,
Put them in, give it a stir.
Double, double, smells of trouble,
Make the teachers into bubble.
Add the hairy Alban owl,
Add the teacher's swimming towel.
Double, double, smells of trouble,
Make the teachers into bubble.
Paint the cauldron black and green,
Make a fancy, scary scene.
Double, double, smells of trouble,
Make the teachers into bubble.

*Sophie Noble (11)*
*St Alban's RC Primary School*

## MACBETH

Trouble, trouble, get rid of school,
Throw it away, it's so not cool.

Throw in a dash of teacher's glasses,
Fresh from looking into classes,
Add a word from teacher's board,
And a rivet of our toad.
Don't forget a pointless book,
Lumpy custard made by cook.

Trouble, trouble, get rid of school,
Throw it away, it's so not cool.

Steps taken slowly by our teachers,
Boring, gory, science features,
Quiet lines we must stand in,
Nightmare memories thrown in the bin,
Wasted money spent on time wasting trips,
Trying to watch boring, old ships.

Trouble, trouble, get rid of school,
Throw it away, it's so not cool.

*Laura Clifton  (11)*
*St Alban's RC Primary School*


## SWIMMING

Every Friday I go swimming
I put my trunks and goggles on.

I swim with my woggle, and I lost my goggles,
While I dived in and grabbed a fin.

*Dean Hall  (9)*
*St Alban's RC Primary School*

# LEAVES

Leaves
are yellow
Leaves are so
very colourful.
Orange is like fire.
Leaves come dancing down
Leaves can be red, amber,
brown and orange. Leaves
blow off trees and make a rattling
sound. If you kick them they will scatter
all over the place. Leaves are green
every month except from
October. Leaves are red,
amber and yellow
and orange.

*James Charlton  (7)*
*St Alban's RC Primary School*


# FALLING LEAVES AT AUTUMN TIME

Leaves
dancing
down, reds,
browns, ambers,
oranges, golds, yellows.
shiny and bright. While
the leaves are dancing around
softly and twisting, silently and
slowly. All going low to the ground
more and more, bright and crunchy.
Let me see if I can hold them.

*Laura Ogle  (8)*
*St Alban's RC Primary School*

## OUT OF MY WINDOW

Out of my window on a sunny day
There are children playing as happy as Larry
Out of my window on a sunny day
I see the ice cream van coming this way.
Out of my window on a windy day
The leaves on the trees dance in the breeze.
Out of my window on a windy day
The children are wrapped up as cosy as can be.
Out of my window on a rainy day
There's no one outside except for cars going by
Out of my window at night
Stars are twinkling
The moon is bright
Everyone's asleep
So . . .
Night-night.

*Claire O'Sullivan (8)*
*St Alban's RC Primary School*


## LEAVES

Leaves
are yellow
Leaves are very
colourful. Orange is
like fire. Leaves come
dancing down. Leaves
are playing tiggy
and giving the
ground its
crown.

*Ellie James (8)*
*St Albans RC Primary School, Walker*

## UP IN THE SKY

Up in the sky there's a famous guy,
And his name is God.
He's odd from all the rest
Because he wears a raggy vest.

Angels are in the stars
They might be able to see Mars
I like angels, they're quite sweet
And I think they're quite neat.

The sky is blue
I love the colour too
I look above at the sky at night
Of course it wouldn't be light nor bright.

*Linzi Moran  (9)*
*St Alban's RC Primary School*


## LEAVES

Leaves swish silently to the ground
Making a kind of swirling sound
Twirling around in the autumn breeze
Blowing silently through the trees.

Scattered and separated from the branch
Crunched and curled, locked up tight
Through the night skies burn bright.

Leaves glide away in the autumn days
While foxes go and catch their prey.

*Joseph Emmerson  (7)*
*St Alban's RC Primary School*

## OUT OF MY WINDOW

Out of my window,
On a bright, nice Sunday morn,
The children are playing like little puppies,
The day is as nice as dawn.
Out of my window,
Nice in the Monday breeze,
You want to go out,
It is quite a tease.
Out of my window,
You'll hear me again,
The children playing like kittens,
All over the lane.
Out of my window
On a bright Wednesday,
You'll hear the ice cream man.
Coming this way.
Out of my window,
On a bright Sunday morn,
The children are playing like little puppies,
The day is like dawn.

*Emily Kerr  (9)*
*St Alban's RC Primary School*


## WONDER WHY?

I wonder why the sky is blue?
Why isn't it green or other colours too?
I wonder why the sun is so bright?
Or why does the moon shine all through the night?
I wonder why people at night get tucked in so tight?

*Abbie Cairns  (9)*
*St Alban's RC Primary School*

## WINDY DAY

The wind can blow and push you,
The wind can blow branches off trees,
The wind is very strong
The wind can be horrible and cold
The wind can blow your coat open
But sometimes the wind,
Can be
Gentle.

*Alfie Stanley (8)*
*St Alban's RC Primary School*


## TEACHERS

Teachers are cheeky
Teachers are boring
Teachers are understanding
Teachers are fast
Teachers are slim
Teachers are smart.

*Jamie Callaghan (9)*
*St Alban's RC Primary School*


## LEAVES

Leaves swish and dance, bring colours
Leaves twirl, spiral, crunch softly near your feet
Leaves tumble, spin, blow.

*Louise Douglas (7)*
*St Alban's RC Primary School*

## SCHOOL

School is a place
Where I have to go
I learn a lot
And have some breaks
Then back to work
After school the day has ended
I go to bed
Then tomorrow
I do the same.

*Blaine Tiplady (9)*
*St Alban's RC Primary School*


## THE MOON

Shining bright in the night
Sleeping dogs with silver claws
I walk the night in a silver cloak
Visible at night
Invisible at day
What am I?
The silver moon above.

*Daniel McGonagle (10)*
*St Alban's RC Primary School*


## LEAVES

Leaves, sunset colours
Fall from trees.
Autumn. Rustle when stood on.
Leaves dance from trees.

*Robert Humphries (7)*
*St Alban's RC Primary School*

## LEAVES

Fall is here, fiery leaves and bare trees.
Twirling and twirling round and round
Without a single sound.
Dancing and dancing again and again.
Dashing and dashing down.
Fall is here
Colours of fire-red and orange,
Yellow and gold.
Glowing and glowing every time.
Waiting and waiting until autumn is alive.

*Jessica Robinson  (8)*
*St Alban's RC Primary School*


## THE FOOTBALLER

His football studs are as sharp as a knife
He kicks the ball as high as school
His strike foot is as strong as a bear
The front of his football boots are as pointy as a witch's hat
He runs like the wind
The footballer is as skilled as a professional.

*Robbie Molloy  (8)*
*St Alban's RC Primary School*


## FALLING LEAVES

Leaves fall softly changing colour
from red to brown, amber to orange
gold to yellow, shining bright.

*Charlotte Scott-Graham  (8)*
*St Albans RC Primary School, Walker*

## THE FOOTBALLER

A footballer is as fast as a bullet
He is very strong
He's as strong as a lion
He can kick the ball
As powerful as a jet rocket
His studs are as sharp as a shark's teeth
He can kick the ball straight at the goal.

*Dylan Bratton (8)*
*St Alban's RC Primary School*


## THE ICE SKATER

Their blades are like razors
They wear little leotards
And have hair like golden wire
Their eyes are like the sun
They are fast as a cheetah
They skate on freezing, cold ice
Gliding along as graceful as a swan.

*Laura Drew (8)*
*St Alban's RC Primary School*


## LEAVES

Gold flames watching a sunset through the air
Looking like diamonds shining in the air
Looking like diamonds
Gold, dancing flames.

*Alexander Long (8)*
*St Albans RC Primary School, Walker*

## SWEETS

Sweets are hard
Sweets are soft
Sweets are yummy
Sweets are not
Sweets are red, green, purple
Sweets are long, short and small;
Sweets are round, square and all.

*Sophie Paton  (9)*
*St Alban's RC Primary School*


## LEAVES

Leaves falling, dancing around
Swishing softly, leaves burning
A sunset of leaves all gold, yellow and brown
Scattered everywhere with the wind
Blowing all over the world in the windy air.

*Jordan Laffey  (8)*
*St Alban's RC Primary School*


## STARS

Stars, stars, come out at night
And they are also bright
They twinkle in the night sky
And in the morning they say goodbye!

*Ashleigh Francis  (9)*
*St Alban's RC Primary School*

## COLOURS

The sky is blue,
The grass is green,
The roads are black,
The flowers are white,
The sun is yellow,
Colours are so bright,
And shine in the light.

*Gary McGarrigal  (10)*
*St Alban's RC Primary School*


## COLOURS

Red for blood
Yellow for a flower
Green for grass
Black for death
White is a sheep
Orange the fruit
Let's all make a mess!

*George Douglas  (9)*
*St Alban's RC Primary School*


## HARRY POTTER

Harry Potter is his name
Harry Potter is a wizard
Harry Potter has a wand
Harry Potter has a broom 2000
Harry Potter has a hat
Harry Potter has a friend called Ron.

*Dean Conway  (10)*
*St Alban's RC Primary School*

# A WALK IN THE PARK

You must go to the park
It's as pretty as can be.
The leaves fly as high as the birds
You can have a peaceful walk
Gliding like a swan, swaying along
Watch the children run as fast as the wind.
Sit down and have a picnic,
Eat as much as you like.
The sun is shining bright as bright as a light bulb
Enjoy the sun
The park is fun.

*Amy Mitford (8)*
*St Alban's RC Primary School*


# HARRY POTTER AND JACQUELINE WILSON

I like Harry Potter
Because he is so funny
He is a wizard
And he has got an owl
I like his books.

I like Jacqueline Wilson
Because I like her books
She is so funny.

*Charlotte Devine (10)*
*St Alban's RC Primary School*

## THE ICE SKATER

She spins like a spinning top up in the air,
She will never stop,
She has a dress as pretty as the twinkling stars,
Her shoes are as white as salt,
Herself skating as quiet as a mouse,
She is as hot as fire,
And as wonderful as can be.

*Taylor Moorhead (9)*
*St Alban's RC Primary School*


## LEAVES

Leaves swish, leaves fly
Silently onto the ground
Making a kind of swishing sound.
Twirling around in the autumn breeze
Blowing silently through the trees
Scattered and separated.

*Kimberley Carter (7)*
*St Alban's RC Primary School*


## LEAVES

Leaves, red, amber, gold or orange
Yellow and brown fall from the trees.
Softly dancing to the ground.
Kicking leaves and scattering them.

*Jordan Ray (7)*
*St Alban's RC Primary School*

## ENGLAND

E ngland is my favourite football team
N ewcastle stars on the team
G ood players we have
L et's play it with the lads
A nd the cup we will win
N ow let's go beat the Finns
D ummied the keeper, one-nil to us, final score
   we have won the cup!

*Andrew Fisher (9)*
*St Cuthbert's Catholic Primary School*


## SHARKS

S harks are clever
H ungry a lot of the time
A long the shore tiger sharks go
R ain does not bother them
K iller stuff is their thing
S o watch out, they're around.

*Richard Haggath (9)*
*St Cuthbert's Catholic Primary School*


## SOCKS

S ocks are smelly
O r
C lean, so are
K ids -
S ometimes!

*Josh Coles (10)*
*St Cuthbert's Catholic Primary School*

## THE CROCODILE

That crocodile is mean
His teeth are very clean
He's very smart
He looks the part
His skin is green
He's the scariest thing I've ever seen.

He's very shy
And loves to eat pie
His mouth opens wide
He gobbles the food inside
So always beware
A crocodile could be there!

*David Scott Robertson  (9)*
*St Cuthbert's Catholic Primary School*

## FOOTBALL

F   ootball is what I play
O   h no! It's an own goal
O   n the pitch I go
T   o the net
B   elt the ball, and it's a goal!
A   nd now it's 5-1 to *my* team
L   iam's on the ball now, and it's another goal!
L   iam's now scored two goals.

*Liam Alexander  (10)*
*St Cuthbert's Catholic Primary School*

## CATS AND DOGS

C ats are cuddly and they scratch all day
A lways eat all day
T hey sing as well

A nd even cats with a hat will
N ot scare a dog
D on't even think about wearing a hat you silly, silly cat

D ogs, dogs, dogs! They always bark all day
O ooow! When a dog sees me he
G oes, 'Ruff, ruff,' and eats me all up.

*Jordan Tyer  (10)*
*St Cuthbert's Catholic Primary School*

## SILLY NUMBERS!

One wailing wheel was having a meal
Two tall trees fell on their knees
Three thick thieves slipped on leaves
Four fat foxes trapped in boxes
Five foxy fishes were washing the dishes
Six silly sticks liked magic tricks
Seven smelly socks couldn't read clocks
Eight eggy eggs ran around on legs
Nine nutty nuts loved eating guts
Ten terrible teddies ate lots of Shreddies!

*Andrew Hastie  (10)*
*St Cuthbert's Catholic Primary School*

## FRIENDS

F   riends are fun, full of joy
R   elationships can last forever
I   n and out of school together
E   verlasting friendships can go very far
N   ever break up, together, never apart
D   readful fights may also happen
S   oon make up, you're friends again.

*Ashleigh Luke (9)*
*St Cuthbert's Catholic Primary School*


## SCHOOL

S   chool is fun
C   ome because you have to learn
H   old on to school, I want to learn the
O   nly school I like is here
O   nly because I have good friends
L   oving and caring I get at school.

*Samantha Luke (10)*
*St Cuthbert's Catholic Primary School*


## SKOOL EXAMS

In skool exams I'm excelling
So I rote to my mam foretelling
In all results I mite
Be doing quite allrite
But I think I'm failing in speling.

*Cathal-James Sear (10)*
*St Cuthbert's Catholic Primary School*

## FOOTBALL

F   ouling and scoring
O   ff with red cards
O   ver the bar
T   hrough the players' legs
B   ounces in the net
A   t last, five minutes to go
L   osing . . .
*L   ost!*

*Scott McMaster  (10)*
*St Cuthbert's Catholic Primary School*


## TEDDY

T   eddies are cuddly
E   ven day and night
D   ancing and singing
D   oing it right
Y   elling and screaming..

*Neisha Williams  (10)*
*St Cuthbert's Catholic Primary School*


## ANIMALS

Imagine a dog perched on a log
Imagine a cat, round and fat
Imagine a rat hiding under a mat
Imagine a fox hiding in a box.

*Tony Cronin  (9)*
*St Cuthbert's Catholic Primary School*

## PUPPIES

P  uppies are cute
U  nless they play the flute
P  aws are small
P  uppies sometimes fall
I  nside, outside.
E  ars flopping down
S  ometimes they frown.

*Kirstie Elizabeth Boyd (10)*
*St Cuthbert's Catholic Primary School*


## PAUL

Paul was a boy who was cool
He loved to play in the pool
The water turned to ice
He said it felt nice
And now he's cooler than cool.

*Jodie Scott (10)*
*St Cuthbert's Catholic Primary School*


## HAIR

There was a young girl called Clair
Who really wanted long hair
She got all her friends
To pull at the ends
Then there was nothing there.

*Clair Formosa (10)*
*St Cuthbert's Catholic Primary School*

## TREASURE

T reasure means money
R ich I will be
E very piece of money means rich, rich to me
A way, get away, this is all *my* treasure
S o I don't share
U nusual for me - not!
R eally money is all that I like
E vil's my game
S o *you* will share.

*Andrew Foley (10)*
*St Cuthbert's Catholic Primary School*

## FOOTBALL

F ootball is fun
O uch! It can hurt
O ften it doesn't
T ouch, don't push
B ut play fair
A t all times
L et's start this game
L et's finish fair.

*Darren Moore (9)*
*St Cuthbert's Catholic Primary School*

## FANTASTIC FALCONS

Rugby is a wonderful game,
　for some it brings lots of fame.

George, Jonny, Inga and Dave,
　make a team that are so brave.

Conversions, scrums, rucks and maul,
　you can bet Epi comes out with the ball.

Watch out folks, fists are flying,
　George has put someone out lying.

Went to Twickenham, the cup we won,
　and that's just some of what we've done.

*Stephen Wade  (10)*
*St Cuthbert's Catholic Primary School*

## FOOTBALL

F   ans shouting
O   ut loud
O   ver the goal the ball went
T   he ball hit the post
B   ut nobody scored
A   ll the people laughing
L   aughing happily
Losers crying.

*Shaun Spiers  (9)*
*St Cuthbert's Catholic Primary School*

# FASHION

F  is for fabulous
A  is for absolutely fabulous
S  is for small fitting
H  is for hippy trousers
I   is for I love them
O  K! Fashion isn't everything (yeah right!)
N  is for nothing fits.

*Samantha Tyer  (10)*
*St Cuthbert's Catholic Primary School*


# MARY THE WITCH

There was a witch called Mary
She was tall, green and hairy
One day she went through the sky
And got a face full of pie
She couldn't see so she fell off her broom
And landed . . . with a *boom!*

*Sarah Younas  (10)*
*St Cuthbert's Catholic Primary School*


# SHARKS

S  harks are cool
H  ave lots of teeth
A  shark had a bite out of me
R  un, run or swim away
K  illers of the sea
S  harks are very cool.

*Danny McLafferty  (10)*
*St Cuthbert's Catholic Primary School*

## ME AND MY LIFE

I have a terrible life
So boring and blue
If I got sent to my room there'd be nothing to do
My room is the worst, it's decorated black
If I had the chance I would throw it in a nappy sack.
How bad can it get?

*Sophie Jane Murray  (10)*
*St Cuthbert's Catholic Primary School*


## HIDDEN TREASURES

One sunny day a woman died
And there she lies
Hidden treasures in the sea
I heard a voice saying let me be
I heard a voice saying let me be
I went back
Oh, I hurt my knee
I got my fishing rod
Put it in the sea, pulled it out
There was the hidden treasures
There was the hidden treasures

I opened the box
For there in the box was gold
Bt for the box it was all mould
I was very shivery and cold
I put my hand in the box

> There was the hidden treasures
> There was the hidden treasures.

*Megfan Athey  (9)*
*St Paul's CE Primary School*

174

## HIDDEN TREASURE

Treasure is hidden somewhere,
Nobody knows where it is hidden,
I've looked for 25 to 30 years,
But I still have not found it.
I've looked high and low,
Far and wide,
But still it is hidden up there somewhere.
The mountain is high,
Where the treasure lies,
I am halfway up,
But still no sight of the treasure.
I'm three quarters of the way,
But then I fall.
Now I have to start again,
Up the mountain with my little hen.

*Jamie Humble  (9)*
*St Paul's CE Primary School*


## HIDDEN TREASURES

Hidden treasures lost in the sea,
Hidden treasures scattered by a tree.
Hidden treasures found by me,
Hidden treasures everyone can see.

Hidden treasures crashed by a car,
Hidden treasures hit afar.
Hidden treasures I'm lucky to have,
Found treasures all for me and my brother Jake.

*Samuel Ameobi  (9)*
*St Paul's CE Primary School*

# HIDDEN TREASURES

Hidden treasures here
Hidden treasures there
Hidden treasures everywhere
Hidden treasures above
Hidden treasures below
Hidden treasures in
Hidden treasures out
Hidden treasures in the sea
Hidden treasures out the sea
Hidden treasures with people
Hidden treasures without people
Hidden treasures being found
Hidden treasures being burned
    But most of all
Hidden treasures are on ships.

*Steven Gaughan  (9)*
*St Paul's CE Primary School*



# THE TREASURE CHEST

I found a box full of treasure
It made my heart full of pleasure
It could have been a box of heather
But the chest was full to the rim with treasure.

In it were diamonds that glittered in the starlight sky
Also there were beautiful pearls
And a box of dancing robins.

*Henna Javed  (10)*
*St Paul's CE Primary School*

## THE HIDDEN TREASURE

I saw a diamond shining bright
Underneath the bright sunlight
I saw a gem lying on the ground
It must be from the lost and found.

I buried some treasure under a tree
But now it's gone, oh can't you see?
I loved my treasure but now it's gone
I wish I'd never buried it under the gong.

*Cherie Renton  (10)*
*St Paul's CE Primary School*


## HIDDEN TREASURES

Hidden treasure in the sea,
Hidden treasure you can see.
Hidden treasure under my bed,
Hidden treasure in my head.

Hidden treasure is very red,
Hidden treasure in my bed.
Hidden treasure upside down,
Hidden treasure everywhere.

*Nicola McCutcheon  (10)*
*St Paul's CE Primary School*